When I Am Weak,
THEN I AM STRONG

To Casey:

God bless you and your
faithful service in Young Life.

When I Am Weak,
THEN I AM STRONG

Keeping Faith through Adversities

Through Faithful Fortitude,
Pam
Gray

Pam Gray

WestBow
PRESS
A DIVISION OF THOMAS NELSON

WestBow Press books may be ordered through booksellers or by contacting:

WestBow Press
A Division of Thomas Nelson
1663 Liberty Drive
Bloomington, IN 47403
www.westbowpress.com
1-(866) 928-1240

Because of the dynamic nature of the Internet, any web addresses or
links contained in this book may have changed since publication and
may no longer be valid. The views expressed in this work are solely those
of the author and do not necessarily reflect the views of the publisher,
and the publisher hereby disclaims any responsibility for them.

Certain stock imagery © Thinkstock.
Any people depicted in stock imagery provided by Thinkstock are
models, and such images are being used for illustrative purposes only.

ISBN: 978-1-4497-2202-9 (e)
ISBN: 978-1-4497-2203-6 (sc)
ISBN: 978-1-4497-2204-3 (hc)

Library of Congress Control Number: 2011912201

Printed in the United States of America

WestBow Press rev. date: 7/22/2011

Dedicated to

my loving husband, Bob Gray;
my three lovely daughters,
Jennifer Nicole Gray Vonderheide,
Jill Renee Gray Parker, and
Jamie Michelle Gray Bell;
and all my dear friends who labored
through this journey with me.

INTRODUCTION

When I am Weak, Then I am Strong is only a small sample of my memoirs. It will take me at least three books to actually write down how God has worked throughout my life and is now using my stories to witness to others. When my life, as I knew it, came to an abrupt halt at age seventeen, I proclaimed to God that if my condition could be used for His glory, then hopefully He would allow me the opportunity to share with others.

My youngest daughter, Jamie, called to see if she could borrow some of my stories to share with her fiancé. During the same timeframe, I was grieving over the death of a friend who died of Myasthenia Gravis. It was then that I felt the prompting of the Lord saying that it was time to tell my story. So in January of 2011 I began the journey of what is now called *"When I am Weak, Then I am Strong."*

This book is written to share as an instrument to inspire others to lean on Jesus Christ, our Lord and Savior through all aspects of their lives.

You may not see yourself through every myriad of the joys and sorrows in my life, but hopefully you will see how faith in God can help you to find the answers you are seeking.

May you find true blessings in life as you continue your walk with God.

Your Servant and His,
Pam Gray

CONTENTS

"Be joyful in hope,
Patient in affliction,
Faithful in prayer."

Romans:12:12 (NIV)

CHAPTER 1
THE GAME OF LIFE
1973

In August of 1973, I left my home in Indiana for a Young Life camp in Colorado called the Frontier Ranch. It was the summer prior to my senior year in high school. I was a happy, healthy teenage girl, anticipating the time of my life with other campers who shared my faith in God. Little did I know that when I returned home, my life would be changed forever, and I would face the challenge of adjusting to a whole new way of participating in life.

Frontier Ranch was situated in a breathtakingly beautiful part of Colorado. Surrounded by mountains, the camp offered crisp, invigorating air; gorgeous scenery; and a chance for Christian teenagers to be themselves as they enjoyed each day's exciting schedule. We participated in the usual camp activities of swimming, horseback riding, challenge races, and campfires. On our last full day at Frontier Ranch, we were going to climb Mt. Princeton. I was excited! Scaling a mountainside was something I had never done. After all, there are no mountains in Indiana.

We met with the guides to receive our instructions on how to prepare for the climb. We were to wear shoes or boots that had a good grip, long pants, and jackets tied around our waists. There was a possibility of snow at the higher elevations, and it could get rather chilly, even in August.

I was ready. Nothing would do but to climb all the way to the top; besides, there would be a Rocky Mountain High trophy awarded to a camper that night after our return. At the beginning of our climb, I was at the front of the pack. I kept a pretty fair pace for the first half hour or so before I slowed down. Soon, others climbed past me. I stopped to rest. Why was I having so much trouble? I'd always been active in sports. This didn't make sense. My legs began to ache, and it became increasingly difficult to breathe. I'd always heard that the air was thinner in higher elevations, but I never imagined it would be like this.

Eventually, my legs buckled, and I fell down. I was embarrassed, but I wasn't going to let it stop me. I struggled to get up and continue the climb. I had a goal to reach! Wanting to resume my position near the front of the group, I picked up the pace, but I'd only climbed another ten feet or so when my legs collapsed again. Even though I kept trying, my legs weren't strong enough to support me. Each step got harder. One of my fellow campers asked if I wanted her to notify the nurse who'd accompanied us on our hike, but I said no.

I wasn't quite sure why all of this was happening to me. No one else seemed to be having any trouble. I didn't want anything to keep me from reaching the top of the mountain. Several guys who were about to climb past me asked if they could help. When I told them what was happening to me and my goal, they took turns carrying me on their backs as they crawled up the side of the mountain. In spite of their help, my condition continued to deteriorate. My breathing became labored, and I could no longer keep my eyelids open. It was an effort to speak. I was fading fast.

The higher the altitude was, the colder it got. The boys put a jacket around my shoulders to keep me warm. They asked if I wanted to quit, but I wasn't about to quit. They assured me that they would see that I reached the summit. And then I lost consciousness.

The next thing I remember was the nurse calling out my name and asking if I could hear her. When I opened my eyes, I realized I'd made it to the top. I didn't know if I was dreaming or if I actually had reached the top of Mt. Princeton, but the other campers kept telling me to hang in there—that I had reached my goal.

It was an absolutely amazing and beautiful sight! I'd never seen anything so magnificent. The skies were blue, there was snow on the ground, and I could see other surrounding mountain peaks. It was even more spectacular than I had imagined. I breathed a sigh of relief as a true sense of peace and accomplishment came over me. Then I drifted back into unconsciousness.

The nurse sent someone down the mountain to get help. I'm not sure how much time elapsed, but I woke up once again to the realization that I was strapped to a blanket-covered stretcher being carried down the mountain by several paramedics. They kept slipping and sliding as we made the downward trek. Once we arrived back at the ranch, the men laid me on a cot in the nurse's clinic. By this time, my breathing was stable, and I stayed conscious. I asked the nurse what was wrong with me. She didn't know. She told me get some rest. I just laid there until I fell asleep.

Later that evening, I awoke to the sound of clapping coming from the mess hall. The nurse told me they'd just announced that I was doing much better. The camp staff had chosen me to receive the Rocky Mountain High trophy because of my determination to make it to the top of Mt. Princeton.

I was ecstatic to hear that I'd won the award, but so tired that I just wanted to go back to sleep. While I rested, my cabin counselor had a fellow bunkmate pack my bags for the trip home to Indianapolis the next morning. The nurse suggested that I make an appointment to see my doctor as soon as I arrived home.

The next day, we said goodbye to all of our new friends and workers at the ranch. The campers exchanged addresses with each other so we could stay in touch. We loaded the bus for the long ride home. By then, I had a sore throat, and I felt like I was running a low-grade fever. I slept for most of the ride home, thinking I was coming down with the flu.

The twenty-four hour bus ride from the mountains in Colorado to Indianapolis gave me the opportunity to reflect upon my experience at the Frontier Ranch. I'd loved every minute of my Young Life trip. It was awesome to think how those boys had pitched in to carry me up the mountain to be sure that I reached my goal when it had to have been an excruciating experience for them. I met some very special people that week, had a great time, and saw some spectacular scenery. Those had been the best ten days of my life! Our bus pulled in the parking lot, where our parents were waiting for our arrival. From the moment my mother laid eyes on me, she could tell that I was sick. I told her about my muscles giving out while climbing up the mountain and how I'd started feeling sick on the bus ride home. She said she would call our doctor right away the next morning.

Little did I know that what lay ahead would alter my life completely. I'd gone to camp that August as a wide-eyed teenager with the entire world before me—a happy, healthy girl who led a very active lifestyle. Anything seemed possible, and opportunities were limitless. I had great expectations! The news I was about to receive would convert me from active participant to spectator. The plans and goals I had for my future would soon be distant memories.

CHAPTER 2

A MOUNTAINTOP EXPERIENCE COMES TUMBLING DOWN

1973

On Monday morning, my mother called the doctor's office as soon as it opened. She was able to get me an appointment to see Dr. Martin later that afternoon. He examined me and ordered lab work, handing my mother the list of the tests he was ordering. I was to go right home from the lab and stay in bed until he called with my results.

Since I slept most of the time, one day seemed to blend into the next. Instead of getting stronger, I continued to grow weaker. Eventually, I needed help just to walk to the bathroom. *Why wasn't I getting any better?*

When the test results came back, Dr. Martin called to say I needed to have some more tests run. He thought I had some type of virus. Mom and I waited for my dad to get home so he could help carry me out to the car, and then he drove us to the lab. Again, we waited for the results. I wasn't improving, so I spent most of my time in my room. My mother decided to make up a bed for me on the living room couch so I could watch television whenever I was awake. It also made things better when company came to visit me. She set up a TV tray next to me, so most anything I would need would be within my reach.

The most exciting part of my day was when mother brought me the mail. I received many letters from the campers I'd met in Colorado. Any time a visitor came over, I told them all about my wonderful trip to the Frontier Ranch. Mother had my photos developed. I couldn't wait to show them off, along with my Rocky Mountain High trophy. The whole trip had been fantastic! Even though I was weak and tired, emotionally, I was high on life. I couldn't imagine things getting much better than my experience at the ranch! The camp itself had been great, but being surrounded with lots of new friends who shared my faith in God made it a mountaintop experience!

My mother talked to Dr. Martin several times that week, but the only thing that happened was that I went to have more blood drawn. I figured it was as I thought—a really bad case of the flu—and it would just take time to get better.

My sister, Jackie, who was a nurse, called to see if it would be okay if she stopped by our house that evening after work. I didn't think too much about it until she walked in the room holding a present for me. I couldn't imagine why she was bringing me a gift when she had always told me that I was a pest and that she hated me. I unwrapped the present to find the most beautiful blue robe. It was at that very moment I knew I was probably dying. My sister would not have spent her money on me if she thought I just had the flu.

Many days, I was so weak that I couldn't bathe myself or brush out my hair. I continued to be full of questions but didn't get many answers. Why was I not getting any better? Shouldn't I be starting school? More blood tests again? What is wrong with me?

One of the camp counselors sent me a letter which ended with the scripture of Romans 8:28: "And we know that God causes all things to work together for good to those who love God, to those who are called according to His purpose" (NASB). That Scripture resonated with me that day and has stuck with me ever since. It impacted my life, and I came to know that God had a hand in every part of my life—even in my illness—and He would use it for good.

September 11 was my parents' twenty-fifth wedding anniversary, and they had been planning a trip to Hawaii for as long as I could remember. My mother asked my sister and her husband if they would stay with me at the house while they were gone. Colleen, a nurse who was renting a room at our house, would also be there whenever she wasn't at work.

What I didn't know at the time was that my mother wanted to cancel their trip because of my health. My doctor told her that if she cancelled, I would sense how bad things were, and I might give up. He could see how my spirits were high after my Young Life trip, and he knew that my attitude was making all the difference in keeping me alive. Dr. Martin stated that he would normally put a patient in the hospital during a critical time like this, but since I essentially had two private nurses at my beck and call, I got to stay home. The doctor wanted to keep things as normal as possible for me.

It made me mad when the phone rang and whoever answered it would step into the next room to talk. Why won't they talk in front of me? If I didn't start school soon, then I won't be able to pass my senior year. I was already almost four weeks late in starting the fall semester. I wondered why I was not getting any stronger and why people were being extra nice to me.

When my parents arrived home from their trip to Hawaii, I had another appointment with Dr. Martin. I was determined to get some answers this time, but nothing would prepare me for what I was about to hear. I just wanted some medicine that would get me up on my feet, back to school, and allow me to be active again. I wanted my life back!

I didn't even give the doctor a chance to speak when I started asking him questions. "When am I going to be strong again? When will I be able to drive? How soon before I can start school? How long must I stay in bed?"

Dr. Martin looked very serious that day as he held a bottle of medicine in his hand and proceeded to make this statement: "I want you to take this medicine, and I hope it doesn't work." I thought that was the strangest thing I had ever heard come out of a doctor's mouth. What did he mean when he said he hoped it didn't work? Why wouldn't I want the medicine to work? I wanted to be well. I wanted to be focusing on the dreams for my future.

Dr. Martin explained that if I felt better with this particular medication, it meant I had myasthenia gravis. (MG) I had never heard of that diagnosis before, so I wasn't sure what that meant for me.

We drove home and ate our dinner. After eating, I was to start taking the new medication. In less than an hour, I could tell a big difference. I was able to walk more steadily. I went into the bathroom to take a shower and wash my hair. It was wonderful! I was thrilled to feel like being up and out of bed. I thought the family would be excited to see me up walking around and doing things for myself. No one was saying anything about it, but my thoughts started racing. I thought about all the things I'd be able to do again. I went to my bedroom that night and began answering some of the letters I had received over the past several weeks.

While I was excited to be regaining my strength and feeling better each day with this new medicine, my family still appeared gloomy. That night, after dinner, my parents asked if they could speak to me. My mother finally shared with me everything Dr. Martin had been saying about my health since I came home from camp. He first thought I had leukemia, and that is why they kept taking all the blood tests. Then she told me that I did have some type of viral infection, but there was more. My mother was crying so hard that she could barely get the words out. "Dr. Martin is sure that you have myasthenia gravis." I didn't know what myasthenia gravis was, but it was obvious that it wasn't good if my mother was that upset.

It was all adding up. When my sister gave me that beautiful blue robe, she knew how sick I was. Along with all this information and the diagnosis came a flood of emotions. I was angry, sad, and overwhelmed. Why hadn't they told me anything before now? This was my life, and I had a right to know what was going on! I wasn't about to sit there for one more minute. I grabbed my car keys and ran out the door. I jumped into my car and sped over to my sister's apartment. I wanted to look through her nursing books. Maybe I could find something in there on myasthenia gravis. I looked in her kitchen drawers and found a piece of notebook paper and a pencil. I opened the book and proceeded to write down what her medical dictionary had to say about MG.

MYASTHENIA GRAVIS: (According to the Medical Surgical Nursing book of 1970, second edition, pages 888-889. Lippincott Publishing) A chronic disease characterized by muscular weakness, thought to be caused by a chemical defect at the sites where the nerves and muscles interact. There is some evidence that the disease has an immunological basis.

People with myasthenia gravis find that certain muscles feel weak and tire quickly on exertion. Muscles frequently affected are those of the face, eyelids, larynx, and throat. The patient may first detect the onset of myasthenia gravis by the drooping of eyelids or difficulty in such a relatively simple operation as chewing or even perhaps swallowing water.

There is no true paralysis of the muscles, and usually, they do not atrophy. Severe forms of the disease, however, can be seriously disabling or even fatal, because the vital muscles of swallowing and breathing may be affected.

Both medical and surgical treatments are helpful to many patients. Certain drugs have been used successfully to reverse the disordered chemical reaction at the myoneural junction. Removal of the thymus has also been found effective in some instances.

CARE FOR THE MG: During acute episodes of myasthenia gravis, the patient must be watched closely and his every need anticipated. He may not be able to call for help or do anything to help himself. Severe muscle weakness throws him completely at the mercy of those assigned to his care.

I was completely numb after writing down the description of myasthenia gravis. Was I going to die? Why didn't they tell me? I had a right to know. I sat on the floor and cried. I went from being angry to wondering what would become of my life.

The next several months were tough. It seemed like the doctor's office was turning into my second home. Dr. Martin had a hard time getting my medicines regulated, and I still got tired after being up only a few hours.

I started school, but I had many lessons and much homework to catch up on. The teachers worked patiently with me and tried to be compassionate, but it was a long haul. Luckily, I had completed many of the heavy requirements for graduation in the earlier years of high school. I only needed to take four classes each semester to complete my senior year.

I wanted to set a new goal for myself. None of my other goals seemed obtainable anymore, but I desired to be able to receive my diploma at the same time as the rest of my classmates.

After school each day, I would go home and go back to bed. I still had hours of homework to do in the evenings. All that extra schoolwork was exhausting, but the toughest part was the emotional adjustment to all the changes in my life. Nothing was the way it used to be. I couldn't participate in the same activities I did prior to coming down with this dreaded muscle disease, and I did not want to be a spectator in life!

Wasn't there something more that could be done? Dr. Martin informed me about an MG specialist who might be able to help. The specialist was practicing in Indianapolis. His name was Dr. Tether, but it would be very hard to get an appointment to see him. He was the only doctor in the United States who saw patients for this one particular condition—myasthenia gravis.

My boyfriend, Bob Gray, had a check-up with his family doctor to get his college entrance physical. During his appointment with Dr. Tuchman, Bob told him how I was diagnosed with MG. Dr. Tuchman said that he was familiar with that condition since his good friend, Dr. Tether, was a specialist in that field. The two of them often went deep sea fishing together. Bob's doctor personally called Dr. Tether and booked me an appointment to see him right away. What are the odds of this happening in the natural world? God definitely had His hand in all of this.

I was very excited to have the opportunity to see Dr. Tether. I felt like I was in *The Wizard of Oz* and was asking for muscles. The doctor's office sent me a questionnaire to fill out and bring with me when I came for my appointment. Dr. Tether looked over my paperwork and talked to me briefly, but he wanted to get right to the exam. I'd never been through such an examination before. He gave me several different strength tests to see how long my muscles would hold up before wearing out. Afterward, I felt like I had done a day's workout. When all the tests were run, he proceeded to give me a shot to see if it would give me back my muscle strength, but nothing happened. I was very disappointed. Then he gave me a second injection in the opposite arm. This time, my eyes opened wide, and my arms and legs felt stronger. There was a huge difference in the strength over my entire body. It was as if the Wizard had granted me my wish—my muscles!

Mom and I went into Dr. Tether's office to discuss the findings. He told us that he had only given me water in the first injection and a specific medication, tensilon, in the second. This way he'd know that nothing was jeopardizing the results. When my muscles responded with the tensilon, it confirmed that I definitely had myasthenia gravis. Dr. Tether was a gentle man, and he carefully gave me instructions on how to properly regulate my medications and my activities. He encouraged me to believe that I would be able to resume a few of my former activities once we had the medicine, Mestinon, regulated. I needed to rest between activities and not overexert myself. This was my first ray of hope leading to a halfway normal life. He really must have been a wizard—or at least one of God's angels!

I kept regularly scheduled appointments and continued my ongoing education of MG. Dr. Tether believed his patients would respond better if they understood their condition. My life would never be the same, but God had a bigger game plan in mind.

I found this Scripture and have tried very hard to put it into practice: "I have learned to be content in whatever circumstances I am in" (Philippians 4:11, NASB). God truly has a purpose for all things. We must be patient so He can show us what that is. Your current troubling circumstance may be the very thing that God will use to help you minister to others in the future. Had you not gone through this situation, you wouldn't be able to comfort others by letting them know that you understand exactly what they are going through. The Bible states in II Corinthians 1:3–5, "All praise to the God and Father of our Lord Jesus Christ. He is the source of every mercy and the God who comforts us. He comforts us in all our troubles so that we can comfort others. When others are troubled, we will be able to give them the same comfort God has given us" (NLT). To God be the glory!

CHAPTER 3

LEARNING A NEW WAY OF LIFE

1974

Myasthenia gravis was ever-present in my life, but I attempted to carry on as normally as possible. There were good days and bad days. There were days of accomplishment and days where I stayed in bed to regain my strength.

At seventeen, I did not fully understand God's allowing of such a thorn in the flesh as this. I know that all things work together for good for those who love the Lord and are called according to His purpose, but how could having myasthenia gravis be a good thing, let alone be used by God?

I wanted life to be fun, and this wasn't exactly my idea of fun. I got embarrassed when I held a Coke in my hand and my muscles collapsed, spilling my drink all over the floor. It seems I was cleaning up one mess after another. As a teenager who had been highly competitive, I must have looked like a bug that was easy to squash. Not only was it difficult to endure whenever my muscles collapsed, but it was downright humiliating. Whenever I knew that I was in a weakened state, I did not go out in public if at all possible. I never wanted others to see me like that.

If I talked too much at the dinner table, my facial muscles became so tired from eating and swallowing that I would choke. Simple, everyday tasks turned into a challenge for me—even just trying to chew gum. Brushing my long, black hair became painful. When my friends chose activities that involved climbing stairs, I would either have to decline the invitation or sit at the bottom of the stairs and wait for their return.

As I became more educated about MG, one of the things I learned was that it was not advisable to take hot baths, as this could cause the muscles to weaken. I also read the material given to me by Dr. Tether that described what would happen if I had a Myasthenic crisis. A crisis happens when a seriously ill MG patient may be unable to breathe or maintain an open windpipe because of muscle weakness. This can occur because of insufficient medication or when the patient has developed a respiratory tract infection or an infection elsewhere. The patient may reach a point of no longer responding to the Mestinon or become insensitive to it. Distinguishing among these possibilities may not be easy in an emergency.

I was just a teenager, so I thought this surely wouldn't happen to me. I thought the people who have a crisis must be a lot worse off than me. I was frustrated with having to learn a whole new way of life. All I knew were athletic activities. I loved to play sports and do things that were competitive. My days of winning were over, and attending college was definitely out of the question. My doctors did not think that I could physically endure walking from class to class on a college campus or the long hours of studying and the rigorous schedule of a college student.

I prayed and asked God what He wanted me to do. I was not talented with my hands, and the doctors didn't want me to go to college. My whole life seemed to be changing before my eyes, and I didn't know what to do. I prayed, "How, Lord, will you ever use someone like me?"

In my daily Scripture reading, I came across Philippians 4:13, which read, "I can do everything through Him who gives me strength" (NIV). "Okay, Lord," I prayed, "you be my strength."

Since I wasn't constantly on the go anymore, I found myself taking more time to listen to others and trying to help them. I needed plenty of rest, so the telephone became a valuable instrument for me. I could expand my world by talking to others and not even leave my bed. Wow, what a wonderful enlightenment!

Dr. Tether continued to regulate my medicine so I could function in everyday activities, such as walking, chewing, bathing, driving, and even brushing my own hair without being in complete pain or exhaustion. I needed to learn to be satisfied being the spectator instead of the participant. God took me out of the game and put me on life's cheerleading squad. No, I could not physically be a cheerleader, but emotionally I could encourage others.

I will not tell you that the adjustment from being the player to sitting on the sidelines was easy or quick. I didn't know how to do anything else. I became extremely frustrated. I knew I had to turn my life over to God and let Him lead.

By New Year's Day 1974, Bob Gray and I had been dating steadily for almost a year when he decided that we were moving ahead with our relationship and wanted to plan for our future. In April, during the last couple of months of my senior year in high school, Bob took me to dinner at the Hansel and Gretel Restaurant in Indianapolis and asked me to marry him. We had met at Allendale Christian Camp in Trafalgar, Indiana when we were thirteen and fourteen years old. We had gone steady off and on, but had been exclusive in our dating over the past year.

My answer was yes, and my family was thrilled! Bob was their perfect choice for my mate. Mother had not approved of another guy I had dated in the past, but she felt that Bob was a great man who would take good care of me. He was employed at Eli Lilly pharmaceutical company and was majoring in chemistry at Purdue University in Indianapolis. Bob was good-looking, polite, athletic, a Christian, a hard worker, and had great respect for my family. What more could parents want for their daughter?

We set our wedding date for the following May. We thought a year would be plenty of time to plan the wedding and save money for a down payment on a house. Since my doctor had told me that going to college would be physically out of the question, marriage seemed like the logical thing for me to do. In the 1970s, you either went to college or got married. I looked forward to being a wife.

It amazed me to think that Bob still wanted to marry me, even though he knew I had myasthenia gravis. I was excited at the thought of getting married, but I had reservations when it came to my health. Would I continue to be stable on my medication, or would my condition deteriorate? I didn't want Bob to be married to an invalid.

Graduation day was soon approaching, and I was ready to get school behind me and start planning for my wedding. The morning of my graduation, I woke up with a fever of 102°, but was determined that I would not miss the opportunity to hear "Pomp and Circumstance" played as I walked into the Ben Davis High School gymnasium and took my assigned seat. I set this as a goal, and I was going to see it through. I would not be defeated.

It had been an extremely rough year as I learned to live with a muscle disease. I desperately wanted to hear my name called so I could receive my diploma. I had worked hard to get to that point. Only nine months earlier, I wasn't sure if I would have the strength to finish my senior year or be able to walk up on the stage with my fellow classmates to shake the hand of our principal and receive that beautiful piece of paper stating I was a high school graduate.

Each and every day was special to me. I was grateful to be able to do things on my own. I no longer took the simple things in life for granted. I was thankful to be able to open my eyes and see the beauty that surrounded me. Each time I lifted my arms or walked around the house, I was aware that the ability to perform these daily functions wasn't to be taken lightly. I gained a whole new passion for life and did my best to help others learn this perspective. Most people do not realize what they have until it is taken from them. During a conversation with a friend of mine, Mike Stovall, he said he could see through me how valuable life was. Then he said, "Pam, God is going to take care of you. I know He is, because He can see how you can help others."

After that evening, I thanked God for my life and professed that if my condition could be used for His glory, that He would allow me the opportunity to share with others. I wanted to make my life count. I would never be a college graduate, but I could specialize in making an investment in the lives of others.

Do you make your life count? We never know how long we have on this earth, but we need to use the time we do have for God's glory. God wants to use you as His instrument. Just say yes!

CHAPTER 4

I WANTED THE FAIRYTALE

1974–75

Our engagement should have been a very exciting time in my life as Bob and I prepared for our wedding day, but a phone call changed all that. One night after dinner, my mother and I were sitting at the kitchen table, going over the wedding plans, when the phone rang. I answered it and said, "Hello."

The male on the other end of the line stated that he had been following me and knew my daily schedule. He declared that he would "get me." I slammed down the receiver, thinking it was a prank call.

The next night, I received a similar phone call. This time, he gave the description of the clothes I wore that day as well as a list of where I had been and who I was with. I instructed him to leave me alone, and I hung up the phone. This was really getting creepy. I kept wondering if this guy was following me with the intention to cause me harm.

The phone calls persisted, and I began to get scared. The caller warned me not to tell anyone. I was frightened and didn't want him to hurt me, so I kept it to myself. One evening, I received the call while my parents were in the room with me, and they insisted that I tell them what was going on. My father called the telephone company the following day to have a tracer put on our phone line. During the time we had the tracer, there weren't any more calls. We removed the tracer and believed the nightmare was finally over.

The following weekend, as I was preparing to go out on a date with Bob, a terrible feeling came over me. I couldn't explain it, but I felt as though something horrible was going to take place. I tried to shake the feeling, but it wouldn't go away. I prayed that nothing would happen to us while we were on our date. I was thrilled when we arrived home safe and sound that evening.

I had a hard time falling asleep that night, as I continued to sense trouble looming somewhere. I couldn't wait to see daybreak. I eventually fell asleep but was awakened by the sound of sirens. There was an ambulance and a police car at a neighbor's house. I didn't get to know what happened until the following morning. News came that a guy in a ski mask had broken into our neighbor's house and had attempted to rape my friend.

All the parents in the neighborhood insisted that the girls use the buddy system whenever leaving their houses. This incident confirmed that this stalker meant business, and he wasn't playing games. By this point, I became internally paralyzed and wouldn't even pick up the mail at the end of our driveway in broad daylight. A friend of mine, John, drove over to my house, picked me up for school each morning, and delivered me right back at my front door each afternoon. Upon getting inside my house, I bolted the door and wouldn't leave until my mother came home from work.

Mother worked out a plan with me that whenever I went out for the evening, I would honk my horn, and she would come to the door to watch me enter the house safely. I felt much better knowing someone was expecting me. Just the sound of a telephone ringing horrified me. I always wondered if "he" was on the other end of the line. Later that same week, I received another frightening phone call, and the caller announced that I would be his next victim. He stated that he was going to rape me and that no one would be able to stop him. The stalker had escaped my neighbor's house before the police arrived.

I was more terrified than ever before. I was his specific target. I began to panic each time I heard a strange sound. I hated being alone. At least on the weekends, I knew I would be with Bob.

Saturday night, as Bob brought me home from our date, we were standing at my front door, talking, when Bob noticed someone standing behind a bush at the side of our house. He told me that he was going to go chase after the guy and for me to go call the police. Bob darted out the door, and I ran to find the phonebook to look up the number to call our local police department. A few minutes later, Bob ran back into our house and told us that the guy was wearing a ski mask and had a car parked around the corner with the motor running. Bob tried to catch up to him in his car, but he lost sight of the stalker's car while he was turning onto a major road out of Chapel Hill, our subdivision.

The police came, but they weren't much help. This particular policeman just wanted to rant and rave about how girls dressed inappropriately and that it was no wonder there were problems with Peeping Toms and rapists. Since we didn't have a description other than dark clothes and a ski mask, there weren't many clues for the police to work with. Bob knew the make and model of car the stalker was driving, but he didn't remember the license plate number. The police weren't inclined to help, so we asked them to leave.

It was a horrible feeling to be trapped within myself and wondering if someone was lurking around the corner, waiting to harm me. I wasn't sure which was worse—having a chronic muscle disease, or the fear of knowing someone was stalking me. It wasn't easy continuing with our wedding plans, knowing this guy was still out there somewhere and had never been caught.

Bob and I purchased our first house a couple of months before we got married. Our home had two bedrooms, one bath, a living room, kitchen and dining room with a full basement underneath. There was a porch across the front of the house and a fenced-in backyard. We were thrilled to be starting our marriage with owning a home of our own.

Our house was located on the south side of Indianapolis. This would make it easy for Bob to drive back and forth to work each day. He decided to move into the house early in order to have it freshly painted and ready for us when we arrived back from our honeymoon. On the Tuesday before our wedding, my friend, Sue, rode with me over to the house so I didn't have to make the trip alone. I didn't want to haul all my belongings over after the wedding, so I thought I would drop them off at that time. The three of us carried everything inside, and we visited with Bob for a few minutes.

We drove back to our side of town, and I let Sue out at her house. I sat in the driveway and watched to be sure she was safe. I only lived a few houses down from Sue, so I didn't have far to go after I dropped her off. I pulled into my driveway and honked the horn as usual to alert my mother that I had arrived home. She came to the front door to watch me as I got out of my car. I wouldn't feel safe until I was inside the house with the door bolted. It had started to rain, and I didn't have an umbrella. I decided to make a run for it, hoping not to get soaking wet, but I slipped and fell. I felt as though I was traveling in slow motion as I went through the air before landing on my knees. The pain was so intense that I couldn't move or get up. Mother managed to pull me up onto the front step and drag me into the house. Once she got me settled on the living room couch, she placed a bag of ice on my knees to help keep the swelling down. She was worried that my legs might be broken, so she decided that I needed to go to the emergency room at our local hospital.

The doctors examined me and ordered some X-rays. There was no sign of a fracture, but my left knee cap was knocked out of place, and the right knee was badly bruised. The doctors wrapped up my left knee tightly to hold it in place. The nurses handed me my release papers to sign and sent me home with crutches, a prescription for pain meds, and instructions on how to care for my knees. They said it would take several weeks for my knees to heal. I tried to keep my legs propped up as much as possible, but there was still plenty to do to prepare for the wedding on Saturday. Friends and family pitched in and ran many of the errands for me.

Upon adjusting to the myasthenia gravis, I feared being in a wheelchair for my wedding day, and I wasn't going to let that happen. However, we had to remove the kneeling bench from the ceremony, since I couldn't bend down. I needed the use crutches to get through rehearsal, but I was determined to walk down the aisle without the aid of crutches or a wheelchair during the actual ceremony. Since I had purchased a short dress to wear to the rehearsal, I borrowed a long skirt from my bridesmaid, Jean Hutzler, so no one could see my bandaged knees. I learned quickly to improvise and be flexible with my plans, since things don't always work out the way you want.

The rehearsal went well, and then the wedding party drove to the south side of town to Bob's parents' home. His mother chose to prepare the rehearsal dinner herself. Bob and I ate dinner and visited with our guests, but excused ourselves so we could talk privately. I presented him with a man's 14-karat-gold cross necklace. I felt this symbolized the Christian marriage we were about to enter. Bob seemed proud to receive such a gift. He gave me two beautiful charms that he had engraved with our wedding date. I said goodnight to my fiancé one last time and drove home. I took some pain medication for my knees and was hoping to get a good night's sleep.

February 1, 1975 finally arrived! Bob and I were excited that his grandmother, Mildred Pace, who was dying of colon cancer, was going to be able to join us for the ceremony. She wore the beautiful red and white robe we gave her for Christmas a few weeks earlier. This would be the last outing she attended.

My myasthenia gravis was stabilized at this time and was in pretty good control with regular doses of the Mestinon. The MG was not going to be a problem on my wedding day. Mom, my bridesmaids, my flower girl, and I went up to the church early to get dressed for the wedding. I put on my beautiful, flowing white gown with its long train and veil. No one would be able to see my messed-up knees. Right before the organist started playing "The Wedding March," I took some pain medicine and held tight to my father's arm to keep steady. Needless to say, we walked very slowly. Any of our wedding guests who did not know about my accident earlier in the week probably weren't able to tell there was anything wrong. Bob held on to me once I reached the front of the church.

The wedding ceremony proceeded according to plan, except for the part where Bob's brother, Tom, fainted in the middle of the singing of "The Lord's Prayer." He fell straight back and hit his head on the pew in the front row of the church. We stopped the wedding briefly to make sure he was all right. After resuming the ceremony and stating our vows to each other, we were pronounced Mr. and Mrs. Robert E. Gray, Jr.

I never received another harassing phone call from the stalker, and to my knowledge, he was never caught. However, I was naïve and thought that getting married would help me to feel secure and live happily ever after. I wanted the complete fairytale! I wish I could tell you that this book was like a Cinderella story, but then it would only be a dream.

CHAPTER 5
MARRIAGE AND CHILDREN
1975

Upon arriving home from our honeymoon we worked diligently getting settled in our home putting away all of our lovely wedding presents. Bob and I had only been married two weeks when we went on a weekend retreat as sponsors for the high school students from our church. I was supposed to sleep in the girl's cabin, and he would sleep in the boy's cabin. This was not exactly the way newlyweds usually start out their marriage, but it was nostalgic for the two of us, since the retreat was being held at the same camp where Bob and I had first met some five years earlier. The inspiration inside the retreat center was fantastic, but the weather outside was cold and dreary.

Within a few days of arriving back home, I came down with a bad cold and throat infection. I went to see my doctor, and he gave me some strong antibiotics. He also gave me specific instructions to stay in bed and to be very careful, since an infection of any kind was extremely tough on a Myasthenic patient. Having MG lowers your immune system, which makes it hard to fight off an illness.

I was too weak to do much of anything, so I wasn't able to tend to the usual household responsibilities with my new husband. Bob called and asked his mother if she would come over to our house to help. This only made me feel worse emotionally. She put the sheets on the bed differently than I did and even put the toilet paper roll on the opposite way. It was strange to have my mother-in-law in my home, taking over my household tasks, when I had only been married a few weeks. It was stranger yet to have my husband announce that his mother's way of doing things was the right way.

To any guys out there reading this chapter right now—this is *not* the way to start a marriage. Don't tell your wife that she needs to do things like your mother. Scripture tells us to leave our parents and to cling to one another. The two of you need to make your own way of doing things. In most cases, things are not black and white, but just a matter of choice as to how to accomplish them. Trust me now, and it will save you a lot of heartache. We had to learn the hard way.

I tried to be grateful for his mother's help and invited Bob's family over for dinner. I baked a beautiful ham with all the trimmings. I was only accustomed to cooking for the two of us, but this was a dinner for ten. I worked hard to prepare a lovely dinner and wanted everything to be just right. Bob and I, his parents, and his six brothers and sisters all sat down in the kitchen. After Bob said the prayer, our guests started passing around the side dishes while I carved the succulent ham into nice, thick slices. Bob piped up and asked me, "What in the world are you doing?" He opened up the pantry, pulled out some buns, and told me to carve the ham into very thin pieces. I couldn't believe that he was going to take the lovely dinner I had worked so hard on and make it into sandwiches. It took everything I had within me to keep myself together and not cry.

There were many other incidents that showed us that we still had a lot to learn about each other. We had known each other for over five years, but life was still full of surprises.

Spring arrived, and all the beautiful flowers burst into blooms, the trees brought forth their new leaves, and the grass became green once again. I loved seeing nature come back to life after a long winter, but it also meant that my hay fever would be right there with it. It was nice to be able to turn off the furnace and open the windows for some fresh air, but soon, all the pollen started to affect my breathing.

I was struggling physically, so I made an appointment with my MG specialist. The first thing he asked was if I had an air conditioner to filter the air. I told him that there wasn't one at our house. Dr. Tether wrote me a prescription for an air conditioner and said that way we would be able to take it off our taxes as a medical expense. He informed me that it was too risky for me to put such hardship on my body and that it was aggravating the myasthenia.

I took the prescription home and showed it to Bob. He thought it was the silliest thing he had ever seen. He didn't think that anyone could medically require an air conditioner and that I must have persuaded the doctor to write the prescription. My husband informed me that his family never had air conditioning, and they all lived without it just fine! Well, I lost my cool, packed my bags, and drove across town to stay at my mother's house so I could be in the air conditioning and get a good night's sleep. Bob went out and bought us an air conditioner the very next day!

We both still had a lot to learn about each other, but in particular, we had to educate ourselves about myasthenia gravis. Other members of the Gray family were not accustomed to anyone in their family being sick, except for Bob's maternal grandmother, who had cancer. To them, cancer was an acceptable illness, but not a condition like myasthenia gravis. They did not understand how it was possible for someone to have full strength one day (or hour) and be completely weak the next. This put a strain between my mother-in-law and me. She actually seemed to get angry with me, because she thought this put too much responsibility upon her son whenever I was physically unable to complete a household chore myself. She didn't think it was fair to him. Little did she know that later in her life, she would be calling me for advice about living with MG, as one of her friends was diagnosed with it. Her friend did not survive.

Our first year of marriage was quite the learning experience for both of us. I was still adjusting to life with a muscle disease, and my endurance was just not there. I needed to learn to do things for shorter periods of time and rest in between. I had to be extremely cautious going out in public, where others could be contagious. Having my medication with me at all times was an absolute necessity. If Bob or my family wasn't around, I needed to inform others what to do in case I collapsed and wasn't able to communicate with them. It was emotionally difficult for me to share my medical condition with others, especially strangers who had not yet earned my confidence. More importantly, though, it could be life-threatening to hide my medical frailty from the very people who could help me.

There weren't many people in the 1970s who had heard of myasthenia gravis. Most doctors had never treated a patient with MG and weren't sure what to do themselves. A doctor once told me that it wasn't talked about much in medical school other than barely being mentioned. It wasn't seen that often; or, if it was, it had been misdiagnosed. It wasn't until Aristotle Onassis was diagnosed with MG that more people started hearing about it.

We had been married for about six months when I went in for my regularly scheduled appointment with my MG specialist, Dr. Tether. He put me through the routine of my check-up, and then he asked me a very pertinent question. He said, "How would you like to go into remission?" I couldn't believe my ears! I didn't know there was a way to go into remission. He stated that there was a possibility if I was ready to have a baby. Dr. Tether said that the research physicians now had medical data to support the thought that a pregnant woman who has MG goes through many chemical changes, and therefore, it is possible for her to go into remission after delivering her baby. I was excited and couldn't wait to go home and tell Bob about the news I had learned! We discussed it at length and decided that I should try to get pregnant. We thought it would be great to be young with our children and not have a generational gap. Also, we felt that when our children grew up, we would still be young enough to enjoy life ourselves.

It didn't take long before I became pregnant, and we were thrilled! We wanted to share the exciting news with our families and drove right over to tell his parents, who lived only ten minutes away. When we arrived, Bob's mother was changing the sheets on her bed. We shared with her our exciting news and anticipated that she would be elated. Instead, she informed us that she was too young to be a grandmother and that her youngest child was only five years old, so why would she want a grandchild? This really hit us for a loop, and we were devastated by her response. We kept to ourselves for several weeks to give her time to accept the reality of the pregnancy. The baby was going to come, whether she liked it or not.

Bob decided that he still wanted to tell his Grandma Pace, who lived at his parents' house. We walked into her room and told her of our good news. She was thrilled to learn that she would be having a great-grandchild. Her excitement helped to take some of the sting out of his mother's response. His grandmother didn't live long enough to see our baby, but we were glad that we had the opportunity to share the news with her before her death.

The next day, we shared our baby news with my family, and my parents seemed pleased. My sister had informed them that she was pregnant only four weeks earlier. Both of their daughters would have babies in the spring.

Marriage was quite an adjustment in itself, as we constantly had to consider each other's feelings. Marriage is the blending of two different families who have their own ways of doing things and different personalities, views, finances, outside activities, and beliefs.

It takes time before you realize that just because someone does something different from you; it doesn't make them wrong—just different. After the wedding comes a marriage, and that takes lots of work. There are times when you don't even like your mate, but that is where true love comes in. People who marry should make a commitment to love each other—even when they don't like each other. A biblical marriage is one in which there is total union of two separate lives on the emotional, intellectual, physical, social, and spiritual levels. A solid marriage takes plenty of work; it doesn't just happen on its own.

CHAPTER 6

PREGNANT WITH OUR FIRST CHILD

1975–1976

I was excited to be carrying our first child. There is nothing more fascinating than the wondrous work of God creating a baby inside a mother's womb. I would be host to the tiny infant growing inside me. I couldn't wait until I was showing enough to be able to wear maternity clothes. I went to the mall to shop for my first outfit and found a cute top that read, "I'm not fat, I'm pregnant!" It was bright red with white lettering on the front and an arrow that pointed right to my little bump. I was proud to wear my shirt out in public so the whole world would know that I was with child. I was blessed.

I called my MG specialist to ask for his recommendation of a good obstetrician. He recommended Dr. Shanafelt, since he was familiar with MG and the pregnancy problems that accompany it. Many of Dr. Tether's female patients with myasthenia gravis went to Dr. Shanafelt. I made my first OB appointment when I was a little over two months along in my pregnancy.

My first appointment went well. Dr. Shanafelt thought everything looked good. He told me to be sure that I didn't miss any of my appointments with Dr. Tether during my pregnancy. It would be important for both of them to take care of me.

I was one of the lucky ones who never had any morning sickness, and boy, was I thankful! My sister was also pregnant, and she was having a really rough time of it. I woke up each morning and looked in the mirror at my ever-growing tummy. It was absolutely amazing to think of the miracle of creating a child right there in my own body. God truly gave a special gift to women.

I loved each and every stage of the pregnancy. When I felt the baby move inside me, for the first time, I wept. I could not wait to tell all my friends and family. When the baby became truly active, Bob and I would sit in bed each night and put our hands on my belly just to feel the presence of our child.

My pregnancy was fairly uneventful until I was six months along. I had a sore throat and went into the kitchen to fix myself a cup of hot tea. As I was pouring the boiling water into my teacup, the cup tipped over and burnt my belly. I was in pain and frightened. What if I had hurt the baby? I called my OB doctor's office immediately, and the nurse said that I should go to the emergency room just to be sure. I notified Bob, and he drove me to Methodist hospital. The

ER doctor tended to my burn but assured me that the baby was just fine. I don't know what I would have done if I had caused something bad to happen to my baby.

We started fixing up our second bedroom as the nursery. Bob and I decided to make it a Raggedy Ann and Andy room, since that would work for either a boy or a girl. My mother purchased a new crib for the baby, and Bob spent a Saturday evening putting it together. While I was out shopping, I picked up different decorations to coordinate with our nursery theme.

The last six weeks of the pregnancy began wearing on me. Because of the myasthenia gravis, carrying around the extra weight kept me exhausted. My feet and ankles began swelling and became extremely painful. My muscles collapsed upon hardly any exertion. Dr. Shanafelt asked me to be very careful and not to climb any stairs. I became less and less active and spent more time on the couch with my feet propped up, hoping to keep the swelling down.

Even though I thoroughly appreciated friends and family who gave me baby showers, it was particularly strenuous and rough on me. I did, however, receive many nice and useful gifts, as well as equipment for the baby. I enjoyed looking at them all over again as I opened them for the second time to show Bob in the evenings after each shower. It was a complete pleasure fixing up the nursery in preparation for the baby's arrival.

During the 1970s, there wasn't any method for a doctor to know if you were having a boy or a girl, so you had to decide on names for both genders. We finally settled on Jennifer Nicole for a girl and Jason Robert if the baby was a boy. That way, we were still using the name Robert, since Bob was a Jr. I had studied French in high school, so I wanted to have a French middle name for a little girl, and first names that started with the letter *J* were very popular at that time.

My due date came and went. Each subsequent day filled me with great anticipation, but I also felt somewhat anxious. Two more weeks went by, and my doctor suggested that I go to the hospital to have a stress test run to make sure the baby could withstand labor without any complications. He was also concerned that the baby was growing so large that I would have trouble with a vaginal delivery, since I was such a small-framed woman. Dr. Shanafelt did not want to perform a caesarean section if it wasn't absolutely necessary. It would be much harder for me to recuperate from a surgery than a normal labor and delivery because of the myasthenia gravis.

On Tuesday morning, May 25, 1976, I went to the hospital to run the stress test. The results showed that everything was fine. Dr. Shanafelt asked me if I would like to deliver my baby that day. Bob and I were excited to think this was actually going to be the day that we would bring our first child into the world. The doctor broke my water, and I soon went into labor.

The contractions seemed intense almost from the beginning. The nurses kept a close watch on me because of the affect the labor was having on the MG. Normally, doctors don't want women in labor to have anything to eat or drink, but I needed to have some protein to take along with my Mestinon to keep the MG under control. Someone from the kitchen brought me a carton of milk.

When I was only dilated to two centimeters, the pain was so intense that my blood pressure shot up over 200. The nurse notified Dr. Shanafelt, and he ordered an emergency epidural to be given right away. My body was not tolerating the pain, and they were afraid that I would either have a MG crisis or a stroke. It took the anesthesiologist two tries to get the epidural into my spine correctly. Once in, it took the edge off of the pain and helped my blood pressure to come down, but it also slowed down my contractions.

After twelve hours of labor, I came to complete dilation, and I was wheeled into the delivery room. The pushing was harder on me than the labor, but at 10:31 p.m., Jennifer Nicole was born. She weighed eight pounds and four ounces and was 21¾ inches long, with a dark complexion and lots of black hair. I barely got a glimpse of her when the nurses whisked her off to the neonatal ICU, where they placed her in an incubator. Yes, this eight-pound baby girl was put in an incubator. She was to be observed closely for the first thirty-six hours to be sure there were no signs of myasthenia gravis. They watched her ability to suck, her breathing, and the ability for a nice, loud cry. All these were signs of her muscle strength.

Since Jennifer was put into the special care nursery, they could not allow her to come to my room. The labor and delivery had been so taxing on me that I hardly remember the next forty-eight hours. I was too weak to go down to the nursery and see my newborn until she was two days old. My nurse said she would push me in a wheelchair so I could go down to the nursery to see my baby. It was a very emotional time for me, but I was thrilled to have the opportunity to see Jennifer for the first time since she was born. The nurses took me inside to a separate room where I could sit and hold my baby. I was so weak that a nurse assisted me so that I wouldn't drop Jennifer.

Jennifer was in good health, but I had to stay in the hospital for five days to regain my strength and gain control of all my muscles. The delivery had taken such a toll on me that I was catheterized until the fourth evening. I was relieved that my baby did not show any signs of inheriting myasthenia gravis. I never wanted my children to have to go through the limitations that MG puts on one's life.

On Sunday, May 30, Jennifer and I were both released from Methodist Hospital, which was located right off of 16th Street in Indianapolis. We hadn't given much thought to the fact that this was race day. All our focus was on our new baby and the fact that we got to go home. As Bob was driving us home, we got caught in all the traffic leaving the Indianapolis 500 race track. It took us over four times longer to get to our house than it should have, but our little family of three was home at last!

Jennifer was beautiful and became the center of my life. What could the future possibly hold in store for our little family? I beamed with joy and only had thoughts of wonderful things that could be in our future. Just as my MG specialist had suggested, I went into complete remission for about eleven months. Those eleven months were heavenly! It was a relief not to need to take any Mestinon during that time and still have fairly normal strength. I was blessed to spend the first year of Jennifer's life without enduring any health issues.

Have you ever reached a plateau in your life where you were at a level of contentment? It is nice to know that God gives us periods of rest and revival after going through some rough spots. I like the poem entitled "Footprints in the Sand." It is comforting to realize that our Lord carries us at times to relieve us of our burdens. What a glorious God He is!

My senior picture, August 1973

Mt. Princeton in Colorado

Me with my Rocky Mt. High trophy

Our wedding, February 1, 1975

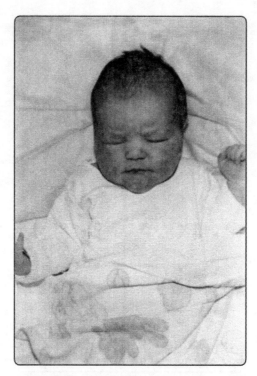

Our first child, Jennifer Nicole

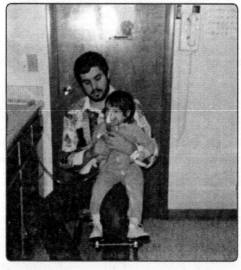

Bob gives Jill a breathing treatment

Jamie's (center) first day of school with her sisters

Daughters: Jill (L), Jennifer (C), and Jamie (R)

CHAPTER 7
KEEPING THE FAITH
1977–1979

Each summer, during the first week of August, Bob attended a special men's retreat called The Northmen that took place in Michigan at an old army barracks. The men brought their own camping equipment, food, and supplies. Not many of the men would go through the trouble of shaving during that week, but if they wanted to bathe, they had to jump into the river to wash off. The men were to endure physically during the week while being fed in-depth spiritually. This was quite a highlight for Bob each year, and it always amazed me to see the revival within him.

The August after Jennifer's first birthday, Bob came home from The Northmen with a new outlook. It was as if the whole world had opened up to him, and he had a true desire to go to Bible college to better equip himself to share Jesus with others. It was too late to enroll for the fall semester, but this gave us time to research Bible colleges and sell our home, boat, truck, and camper in order to be ready to start classes in January.

I am sure people wondered why we would make all these changes at one time. Not only were we selling the house that we had just purchased two months earlier, but we would be moving over six hundred miles from our families for the first time. Bob would be required to take a leave of absence from Eli Lilly, which meant that we no longer had any health insurance or benefits.

When I married Bob, I thought he would always work for Eli Lilly and climb the ladder of success. Eli Lilly was known as *the* company to work for in Indianapolis. It was not easy to get your foot in the door at Lilly, and Bob already had a job there. We were both born and raised in Indianapolis, so I figured we would always live there. Nothing else had ever entered my mind.

I guess we were so busy conducting our lives in the way we thought they should go, we hadn't left our hearts open to God's direction and guidance. Little did we know that this would be the first of twenty-some moves in our marriage. It is much better when you say, "Here I am, Lord, use me," and let Him guide you to wherever He can use you best to accomplish His will.

Change in itself is a major stress factor. Everyone cannot easily adapt to new surroundings. For some, moving can be a tremendous challenge. You must leave familiar territory and friends. Usually, one or both mates start new jobs or positions. Many times, children have to change schools, as well as churches and youth groups. A long-distance move means finding new doctors, banks, cleaners, and drug stores. You become the new kid on the block and need to find your place of acceptance in your new location. With each move we made, it became a little easier the next time, but the first move was indeed the hardest. We found ourselves in a whole new ballgame, and we knew none of the rules.

It is amazing what God can do when you leave yourself open to His teachings and honor His will instead of imposing your own. This began a whole new adventure of learning firsthand what it meant to have *faith*.

My first lesson in faith was learning to trust my husband and his love for the Lord. He wanted to follow Jesus with all his heart, and who was I to stand in the way? There were many times when I humanly wanted to question if we were doing the right thing by going off to Bible college. We prayed to let God know that we were available and wanted to be used as His instruments. We wanted to witness to others and make an investment in their lives for Christ. We proceeded on with our plans to let God open and close doors accordingly.

Before heading off to Bible college, I needed surgery to remove a cyst on my left buttock. It had grown so large that it was visible through my pants. The cyst had grown from a six-inch bruise I obtained from a sledding accident. While zooming down the giant, snow-covered hill, I hit a rock and went flying into the air. I landed on my left side. I was able to stand up, but knew I had hit so hard that I was probably injured. When I arrived home from sledding, I looked in the mirror to see the damage. Nothing appeared broken, so I never said anything until it became obvious that there was something wrong. I went to the doctor, and he said that the impact must have been so hard that it actually destroyed the tissue. The dead tissue then formed a cyst. I needed to have surgery to remove it while we still had medical insurance. The operation went well, but the doctors wouldn't release me to travel for three weeks. When it was time for Bob's classes to start, he had to make the move by himself. Jennifer and I would follow him at a later date.

We researched several different colleges but made the decision to attend Ozark Bible College (OBC) in Joplin, Missouri. Bob contacted the school to see if they had any married student facilities available. The campus had a married student trailer court, but all the homes were personally owned by individual families. There weren't any for sale at that time. We knew that we had been led by God to go to Bible college, so that meant trusting Him to find housing available for us in time for the semester to start.

Less than two weeks before the semester was to begin, we still had no idea where we would be living at college, and our house in Indianapolis had not sold; yet we continued with our plans in faith. One evening, we received a call from an OBC administrator to inform us that one of the married families on campus had decided not to continue for the second semester and needed to sell their trailer. Bob asked them to inform the family that we wanted their trailer, and we would buy it sight unseen. We knew that God had answered our prayers and had opened the door for us.

Bob started his classes on time and even unpacked all our boxes. After I was released by the doctor, Jennifer and I headed for Missouri. It was strange looking for an address that was written on a piece of paper, since I had never been there before. We pulled the car up into the driveway of the address written on my paper. We got out of the car, walked up to the front door, and knocked. Bob greeted us with open arms and was thrilled that Jennifer and I had finally arrived to join him in Joplin. The house looked nice, and all the rooms were in order. I really appreciated all of Bob's hard work. That was the first and only time where I walked into my new home and all the unpacking had been done for me. We had trusted God, and He provided!

There were many wonderful people who believed in our decision to attend Bible college. They supported us financially as well as prayerfully during our four years in Joplin. But whenever God is getting the glory for the great things He is doing, you can bet that Satan isn't far behind in a scheme to cause conflict. During the next four years at Bible college, Satan would rear his ugly head and try his best to get us to quit, but we were determined not to be defeated.

Within a couple of months, our house in Indianapolis sold, and Bob also acquired a weekend youth ministry at the Countryside Christian Church in Pittsburg, Kansas. Many different families took turns inviting us over for Sunday dinner, but the Nance family pretty well took us in and accepted us as their own. They even took care of Jennifer whenever we needed someone to watch her while we took the youth group on outings. It was wonderful to feel so included in a family, since we lived so far away from our own families. We felt totally surrounded by love and support with the Nance family. This was a true ministry for them, and God used them wisely. They are a very special family and will be remembered in our hearts always.

The Nance family would soon learn about my myasthenia gravis. I shared with them what to do in case of a problem. I didn't have an extremely rough time during those four years with MG, but I would occasionally overexert myself and collapse. I kept regular appointments with a doctor and took my medicine as prescribed.

My next big lesson in faith was to trust God with our finances, as the money coming in didn't always pay our bills, and we had no insurance. Bob, Jennifer, and I stayed pretty healthy during this time, so not having insurance didn't really affect us much until I got pregnant again. We had been trying to conceive for over two years. I didn't want Jennifer to be an only child and prayed that God would bless us with more children. Before we were married, we both said that we would like to have three children, but I was having trouble conceiving. I was under the care of Dr. Borello, and he had put me on fertility pills to see if that would help. We really wanted a baby but prayed that it would be a single birth. Bob had twins on his side of the family, and I had both twins and triplets on mine. We thought surely God would only bless us with one baby, since He knew of our financial situation.

Each month, I would get disappointed when I found out that I wasn't pregnant again. I went through this for several more months, each time thinking this would be the moment for a positive pregnancy test, but it was to no avail. After being on the fertility pills for five months, I went in for my scheduled appointment with my OB-GYN, and the nurse ran a pregnancy test, as she did every month before I went in to see the doctor. I had become accustomed to being told that my test was negative again, so I didn't get my hopes up. I prayed that I would accept God's will for my life. The receptionist called out my name and asked that I come over to the office window. I slowly strolled up to see her, and she quickly announced that the results were positive and continued to ramble on about filling out some forms. I asked her to stop for a minute until I could soak in that I was indeed pregnant. I was pregnant! She really did say those words! I cannot begin to tell you the joy I felt upon finding out that I was pregnant with our second child. I was absolutely thrilled and went home to write out postcards to mail to all our family members and friends back home to share the incredible news!

Since we didn't have any medical insurance, my OB required that we make monthly payments to cover our bill, and the final payment had to be made on or before my actual due date. We converted one of our bedrooms into an office where Bob could study quietly. We also displayed our bills on the wall and called it our wallpaper. Whenever we earned some money or received some financial support, we would look at the wallpaper and decide which bill we could pay. Sometimes we threw a dart at our wallpaper to help make the decision. Our circumstances weren't always the best, but they were a little easier to handle if we put some humor into the day. We thought, "What is the doctor going to do; not deliver our baby because the bill wasn't paid on time?"

My second pregnancy was a little easier, since I knew what to expect, and I kept busy chasing after Jennifer. I was pregnant during the summer, and we spent many hours outdoors. I put a child carrier on the back of my bicycle so Jennifer and I could go on many bike rides together. I didn't lack for exercise after tending to an active three-year-old.

When I was almost three weeks past my due date, Dr. Borello grew very concerned about the baby. He scheduled me to go to the hospital on October 19—if I hadn't gone into labor before then—to have the stress test run, just like with my first pregnancy. All was well. The doctor decided that it would be okay if I went into labor for a vaginal birth. The only issue was the fact that it was Dr. Borello's partner, Dr. Bopp, who was on call, and I had only seen him twice during my pregnancy. He felt that since I was already in the hospital, he could monitor me more closely rather than send me home. He wanted to keep an eye on the myasthenia gravis. Dr. Bopp never had an MG patient before, so he wanted to take every precaution. He broke my water, and I soon went into labor; but when the labor became intense and he saw how it was affecting me, he got nervous and proposed that he perform a C-section. Bob asked him if the baby was in any danger, and he told us no, but was worried about me and the MG. Bob explained to him that a C-section might seem to be an immediate answer to the situation, but that it would be harder on me in the long run. It takes longer to heal from a surgery than a normal delivery. Since Dr. Bopp could not show that the baby was in danger, Bob refused to allow him to operate.

While living in Joplin, I had been attending a support group for people with MG, and they were having a meeting in the hospital conference room that very night. I was supposed to attend the meeting at 7:30 p.m., but the baby decided to arrive at 7:10 p.m. We had another precious little girl that we named Jill Renee who weighed eight pounds and three ounces and was twenty-two inches long. She had ivory skin and bright blue eyes, just like my mother.

When I got back to my room, I phoned down to the conference room to explain why I didn't show up to the meeting. They were all excited to know that everything was okay and that my absence was due to the fact that I had just delivered my baby. Our support group had been asked to select two people to do an interview on a talk show that aired each weekday morning during the *Good Morning America* show. The segment was called FYI (For Your Information) and would feature a story about living with myasthenia gravis. The group elected me, along with another lady, to go on television and do the interview in two weeks.

I delivered Jill on a Friday evening, and we were able to go home from the hospital on Sunday afternoon. That evening, we were having severe thunderstorms, and the emergency siren came on the television to announce that there were tornado warnings for our area. I started gathering up a few things that the baby and I might need when there was a knock at our door. It was the police telling us that we needed to evacuate the trailer and go to the print shop on campus. We all headed for the print shop and were greeted by several of our neighbors. This wasn't exactly the homecoming I had planned for our new baby, but we hoped we would be safe.

I had bottle-fed Jennifer but was trying to nurse Jill. Since nursing was new to me, I was pretty clumsy getting started. I never imagined that I was going to be required to breastfeed in front of a bunch of people. I looked for a chair so I could sit down, and there was only one available. It was next to a cat who was feeding her six kittens. Boy, does God have a sense of humor!

The storm was extremely eerie, with the howling wind blowing so hard outside those four walls. We weren't sure if we would have a trailer to go home to. I tried to concentrate on my baby, and Bob entertained Jennifer. We stayed in the print shop until we were given word that it was safe for us to leave. We felt blessed to find that our home was spared, but were saddened to hear that the tornado had struck another trailer court only two miles away, where they had quite a bit of damage.

Have you ever been through an experience where you knew that God must have sent His protective angels to watch over you? Perhaps you were spared from a terrible traffic accident or a near-fatal fall. It is in times like these that we are made aware of God's imminent presence. Psalm 91:11 says, "For He will command His angels concerning you to guard you in all your ways" (NIV).

CHAPTER 8
THIRD TIME IS A CHARM
1979–80

They say that the third time is a charm, but scared is how I would describe my feelings upon learning that I was pregnant again when Jill was only twelve weeks old. This baby would be due on Jill's first birthday. We still didn't have any health insurance, and I questioned if I would be strong enough to handle two little ones at the same time. I believe that everything happens for a reason, so God must have allowed this pregnancy for a specific purpose.

There was never a question if I wanted this child; I never thought otherwise. I just wondered about the timing. Bob and I had always planned on having three children, but we just didn't think it would happen so quickly after having such a difficult time conceiving Jill. Now our family would be complete—just a little sooner than we had expected.

Jennifer seemed to enjoy having a little sister and loved helping me take care of her. That spring, we spent most of our evenings watching Bob play softball with our church league. He was the pitcher and thoroughly enjoyed the game. Bob was known for his home runs, but on this particular evening, he hit only a double. He really hustled to get around those bases. It would be close to see if Bob or the second baseman would get to the base first, so Bob decided to slide into second. The ball field was so dry that dust and dirt went flying into the air. The next thing I saw was Bob limping off the field. When he arrived over by the dugout, I walked over and asked him if he was okay. He insisted that it was only a pulled muscle and that he would be fine. When the game was over, we packed up our things and drove home. Bob asked me to draw a hot bath for him so he could sit and soak. Instead of feeling better, his pain increased. I finally convinced him to go to the hospital and have his leg X-rayed.

We drove to the emergency room. Once the X-rays were developed, the doctor informed us that Bob's leg was broken in two places, and he had also torn some ligaments. They told him that the torn ligaments would probably give him more trouble than the actual fractures. This happened to be the same leg on which he had broken his ankle several years earlier, playing basketball. The doctors instructed Bob not to go to work for another six to eight weeks. Bob was concerned about how we would pay our bills without any income.

The spring semester was coming to a close, and we had some decisions to make. Since Bob wouldn't be able to work and we were still paying off the bills for Jill's birth, had another baby on the way, and had a four-year-old who depended on us, we had to do something. We made some phone calls and decided to go back to Indiana to stay with his parents for the summer. They could help me with the girls, and hopefully, I could find some work. We didn't know how God would work this all out, but we did trust that He would take care of us.

Bob's older brother, Joe, drove over to Missouri to help me load up our cars and drive Bob and the girls to Indiana. Not long after getting settled in at the Grays, I was offered a part-time secretarial position at our home church in Indianapolis. Later that same week, I received a phone call from former neighbors of ours who were looking for a house to rent in Joplin for about six weeks. They had heard about Bob's accident and were told that we went to Indiana for the summer. They asked if we would consider letting them rent our house while we were gone. God worked this all out beautifully. Our house payments were covered, I would make enough for the essential expenses, and Bob's parents provided us with our living arrangements while in Indianapolis. Praise the Lord!

Trying to blend families and live out of another person's home was not an easy thing to do, but we were grateful. We did, however, have the best meals. My mother-in-law was such a good cook, so it was hard not to put on a few extra pounds during this pregnancy. They grew a large garden each summer and we all got to enjoy plenty of fresh vegetables.

There were many hardships that summer, but we were also provided with the opportunity to visit with friends and relatives back home in Indiana while Bob recuperated.

After eight weeks, Bob was released from the doctor's care, so we packed up and drove back to Joplin for the fall semester. This would be Bob's senior year, and then he would have enough credits to earn his bachelor's degree. Many people who had good intentions begged us to stay in Indianapolis and quit school after everything we had gone through. They felt Bob should go back to his job at Eli Lilly, where he made good money and would have health insurance again. Their suggestion was for Bob to get our financial situation in order, and eventually, he could return to his studies. We felt determined that God hadn't led us this far into our journey to quit. We only had two more semesters to go. Yes, we were in the wilderness of life, but God was our constant companion. There were many days of clouds and rainstorms, but afterward, there was always a rainbow. We wouldn't let Satan defeat us.

The Adams, neighbors who lived across from us in the married student housing, greeted us upon our arrival at the Ozark campus. It was good to see them, and we let the kids play in the yard, since they had been cooped up in the car for over eight hours. Norman and Mary Lou invited us to join them for breakfast in the morning, since we had been gone all summer, and there weren't many groceries in the house.

The next day, we met them at Shoney's and enjoyed the delicious breakfast buffet. After eating, we drove back to our house, where Bob said he would put the girls down for a nap while I went to the grocery store. I had made a list of all the items we needed and drove to the shopping center. I entered the store, grabbed a shopping cart, and started down the first aisle of fruits and vegetables. The store kept small ice chips under the produce to keep them cold and fresh. After I picked out some tomatoes, I moved on down the aisle toward the lettuce, where I suddenly slipped and fell to the floor. I hadn't noticed any water on the floor, and there wasn't a sign to signify that the floor was wet. I sat there, stunned. Several shoppers ran over to see if I was all right.

I was seven months pregnant and was quite uncomfortable. A man ran to find the store manager to report the incident. Another gentleman slipped his business card into my purse and said that he had witnessed the whole thing and would be glad to help if I needed him. By the time the manager got to me, I started having contractions. He decided to call for an ambulance. He wrote down my information and called Bob to inform him of the accident and ask that he meet up with us at the hospital. In just a few minutes, the ambulance arrived at the grocery store and drove me to the emergency room. My obstetrician's office was notified, and the receptionist said that one of the doctors would be right over to meet us. Once again, it was Dr. Bopp who happened to be on call, so he became my doctor that day.

After examining me and hooking me up to the fetal monitors, Dr. Bopp confirmed that I had indeed gone into labor. This was not a good thing, since I was just seven months pregnant that day. They wanted to stop the contractions, if at all possible, so the baby would have a better chance of survival. There were many things to think about, but my biggest concern was for my unborn child. The doctor only gave the baby a 50 percent chance for survival if born that day.

I endured through six long hours of labor before the doctors were able to get the contractions to cease. Bob and I were scared. It was not time for our baby to be born, and we didn't want to think about our child struggling to survive. We prayed for our baby like never before. I was relieved when the contractions ended, but it seemed strange to go through all those hours of labor but not have a baby to hold afterward. At least I could hold on to the fact that our baby was still alive.

Between the long car trip from Indiana to Missouri the day before and going through labor for six hours, I was extremely drained. Once the labor had stopped, my OB turned his concern toward me and the affect the labor was having on my myasthenia gravis. He felt it was important that I get some rest. He asked me if I had ever taken Seconal. I had never even heard of it before. Dr. Bopp informed me that the Seconal would help me to get the rest I needed to recuperate from the accident and the toll the labor had put on my body.

I swallowed the pill, and that was the last thing I remember until I woke up the following day.

The Seconal had reacted against the Mestinon I was taking for my muscle disease, and it put me into respiratory failure. The doctors worked on me and drew blood gases throughout the night. Since I had lacked oxygen for so long, the doctor informed us that our baby would most likely be brain-damaged. I felt like someone had just ripped my heart out. How could this be happening to us? This was turning into one giant nightmare. I kept hoping that I would wake up, and the past twenty-four hours would only be a dream. I wanted the patience of Job. Weren't we good Christian people who were trying to learn more of God's Word so we could witness to others?

Not only was Bob unemployed and recovering from a double leg fracture, but classes were starting in a few days, and we had no money for tuition. There was no insurance to pay for my hospital stay. We were still paying off the hospital bills for Jill's birth, and we would have the bills for the new baby, too. What was the purpose of all of this?

Don't ever let well-meaning Christians tell you that just because you are a Christian, you will never experience doubt. Even Christ's closest followers weathered doubt. Christ Himself wondered if there would be any other way for our sins to be forgiven except through His crucifixion. God uses these times to teach us many lessons in life, as well as draw us closer to Him. There are periods when we don't always know the answers to situations, but we must trust that God will use them for His glory.

Bad things do happen to good Christian people. This does not mean that God does not love us or that He wants these things to happen. He does, however, hold true to His promises. One of those promises is to never leave or forsake us. Our Lord is right there with us during all of our hurt and pain. He feels that pain with us and wants to comfort us. The event that happens is not what is important, but how we handle the circumstance through Him. We need to look to God for guidance, love, and support.

I can honestly say that working through each occurrence of adversity, I became closer to our heavenly Father. I became a stronger person. As it says in Ephesians 3:16–19, "I pray that out of His glorious riches He may strengthen you with power through His Spirit in your inner being, so that Christ may dwell in your hearts through faith. And I pray that you, being rooted and established in love, may have power, together with all the saints, to grasp how wide and long and high and deep is the love of Christ, and to know this love that surpasses knowledge—that you may be filled to the measure of all the fullness of God" (NIV).

CHAPTER 9
MIRACLES STILL HAPPEN TODAY
1980–1981

I was in the hospital for three days following my accident, being in labor, and going into respiratory failure. Dr. Bopp sent me home to be on complete bed rest until the baby was born. I wasn't supposed to lift anything over five pounds, so that meant I needed help with Jill, who wasn't quite a year old yet. Bob attended classes in the mornings and worked in the afternoons, and I needed someone to help me lift Jill in and out of her crib, as well as her high chair.

The grocery store where I fell had their insurance company inform me that they would pay for a nurse to come to our house and tend to me until I delivered the baby. They would also cover the expenses for the prior three days of hospital bills. That was a relief to our minds, since we didn't have the finances to pay for it ourselves, but we wondered if the store was being so nice to us to prevent the possibility of a lawsuit.

I really didn't want to have a stranger in our house every day, so I asked if they would cover the expenses for a family member to come to Joplin and look after our needs. They agreed. My Aunt Donnie and Uncle Raymond from Indianapolis drove to Joplin to stay at our house for several weeks. This was extremely helpful. I could concentrate on taking care of myself and the baby I was carrying. The longer I was able to keep from going into labor, the more time the baby had to develop properly.

Dr. Bopp requested that I go to the hospital on Tuesday, October 14 to run some tests to check on the baby's progress. I got up early that morning to prepare to be at the hospital by 7:30 a.m. During my bath, I noticed having some light contractions. I had always dreamed of what it would be like to go into labor and tell my husband that it was time to go to the hospital, but once again, it wasn't in God's plan.

Upon arriving at the hospital and being checked into an observation room, I was hooked up to the monitors. They indicated that I was in labor, so Dr. Bopp had me register as an inpatient. A hospital worker wheeled me down to the labor and delivery department. I was assigned to a very nice and comfortable labor room. It looked more like a living room—except the hospital bed. Bob enjoyed the relaxing atmosphere, where he could read a book between my contractions. It was quite ironic that he was reading a book entitled *Where Is God When it Hurts?*

I liked having a telephone next to my bed in the labor room, where I was able to call home and check on Jennifer and Jill.

Bob's sister, Tina, who had come to Joplin for a visit, was staying with the girls. The room's soothing atmosphere was much more relaxing than the plain, white labor rooms of the past.

Since I had been in labor for over six hours just seven weeks earlier, it was strange to be in labor once again. In a little over four hours, I was at complete dilation and delivered my baby. The doctor announced, "It's a girl!" She appeared to be healthy, and we were elated. Praise the Lord—after all our baby had endured, she was alive!

We named our eight-pound, fourteen-ounce baby Jamie Michelle. The nurses took Jamie to the nursery to monitor her for symptoms of myasthenia gravis. She passed all the tests and seemed to be doing fine. Jamie and I only stayed in the hospital for a little over twenty-four hours. Bob drove us home, and we were greeted by two anxious little girls who wanted to see their new baby sister. Jill was thrilled that she received a baby sister for her birthday. I think Jill thought that Jamie was her baby, as she constantly wanted to hold and feed her. Jennifer acted like a little mother and watched over her sisters.

I took Jamie in for her scheduled appointment with her pediatrician. He said that we wouldn't be able to tell if there was any brain damage until later in her development. He wanted us to observe her closely to see if she acquired the proper functions and motor skills at a reasonable rate.

The insurance company discovered that I had delivered the baby, so they wanted to execute an out-of-court settlement for the accident I sustained at the grocery store. We thought that meant they were going to take responsibility for me and the baby. I was informed that they were only going to settle the claims for *my* injuries. The company's representatives stated that the fetus I was carrying inside of me at the time of the accident was not a legal human being and therefore had no rights. They proceeded to inform me that when this child became eighteen and was of legal age, she could file a claim on her own to express damages caused by the accident. It didn't make any sense to me that they would not acknowledge the child growing inside of me, but would acknowledge her after she was eighteen years old.

The designated money given to me could never replace a child or the mental anguish I had endured. The funds helped to pay some bills, but they didn't assure that my baby would be healthy and whole after suffering through the traumatic event of my fall while seven months pregnant with her.

When I took Jamie to her pediatrician's office for her six-week check-up, she appeared to have normal responses, and I was excited to inform the doctor that everything seemed to be going well so far. After the doctor examined Jamie, he said he had something he wanted to discuss with me. He took a tape measure and wrapped it around Jamie's forehead. He went on to explain that a baby's soft spot on the top of his or her skull meant that the bones were open, as they should be. Under normal conditions, the bones were not to close until the approximate age of two. Jamie's bones appeared to already be fused together. Since her bones were sealed off, the brain wouldn't be able to grow, and she would eventually end up mentally disabled. This was the second time that a doctor was telling me that Jamie could end up being mentally challenged. I had heard that before, but I was hopeful that she was going to be okay, since there didn't seem to be any problems since her birth. I followed the doctor up to the front desk, where I checked out, and he set up an appointment for Jamie to see a neurosurgeon. He stated that the specialist would take images of her skull to confirm a diagnosis. If it was deemed warranted, a corrective surgery could be performed.

I drove us home and went inside to share the news with Bob. He hugged me and stated that we would get through this together. We prayed for Jamie, and then we called our family and friends across the country and asked them to pray for us and for God's will to be done. We also informed the dean at the Bible college. The faculty would request prayers on our behalf at the next chapel service.

Bob and I took Jamie in for her scheduled appointment with the neurosurgeon, and he took some X-rays. He went over the X-rays with us very carefully so that we could see for ourselves that her bones were already sealed shut. He said she had a condition called craniosynostosis and explained that there was a surgical procedure that needed to be performed in order to correct the bone condition in Jamie's skull. He told us what to expect from the surgery and how we would need to find people to donate blood on our baby's behalf, since she would require a complete blood transfusion. I would also need to make arrangements for my other children, because it was compulsory that I stay in the hospital with Jamie to tend to her daily needs. We set up the date for the surgery and went home to make the necessary preparations.

There was never a doubt in our minds that we would sacrifice everything to see that our baby got what she needed. We had no idea where the money would come from, but that was the least of our concerns at the moment. We spent hours in prayer for our baby and knew that God would work out everything that was needed for a successful surgery.

Bob thought that he would be able to tend to Jennifer, our four-year-old, but he didn't feel like he could adequately take care of our one-year-old, Jill. We needed to make alternative arrangements for her. As we were trying to make all the preparations, I received a phone call from my mother stating that my Grandma Cox had just died, and I would need to fly home to Indianapolis for the funeral. My sister had just delivered her baby daughter, Jordan, the day before, and my mother wasn't sure if Jackie would even be able to attend the funeral.

In booking my flight to Indianapolis, I discovered that children under the age of two could fly free with a parent.

Bob's mother offered to take care of Jill while Jamie was in the hospital. My mother-in-law donated blood every month and would specifically ask for her donation to be put in Jamie's name so she would get the credit for it. Many of my mother-in-law's other bus driver friends would be willing to do the same thing. When word got around our campus about needing blood donations for our baby, many students went to the hospital to donate in her name. We felt blessed to see how many others were willing to help.

Bob and I were discussing the financial aspect of Jamie's surgery when we received a phone call from a friend to inform us about the Shriners organization. My friend thought the Shriners covered expenses for families in these situations. I contacted the Shriners office and set up a time for them to come to our house to do an interview. Jamie met all of their qualifications, so they agreed to cover all her expenses for the surgery. What a wonderful God we serve! It was another answered prayer!

I packed Jill's suitcase with the clothes she might need for about a month, and packed my luggage with clothes for only a few days, since Jamie's surgery was scheduled for the next Tuesday. Jill and I boarded our plane and flew to Indianapolis. I made sure that Jill was settled in nicely with the Grays, and I spent the next couple of days with my family, attending my Grandma Cox's funeral and visiting with my sister and her new baby.

On my last evening in town, I attended the Sunday evening church service with my in-laws. I was experiencing so many different emotions at one time that I wasn't able to concentrate on the sermon. I was concerned for my baby and her upcoming surgery, plus the fact that I would be separated from Jill for several weeks. I was mourning the death of my grandmother, yet rejoicing over the birth of my new niece. My thoughts weren't clear, and my emotions were all over the place. Several people came up to me to express their concern regarding Jamie and her surgery. They wanted to let me know that they would be praying for her.

I was about to leave the church when a delightful elderly woman asked to speak to me. She was known as a dedicated prayer warrior. As I greeted her, she told me that my baby was not going to need surgery, because God was going to heal her. I just stood there, stunned for a minute, and then thanked her for the kind words of encouragement. It wasn't that I doubted God could heal Jamie; it was that I hadn't been thinking in those terms. We had been praying for guidance and wisdom for the doctors and nurses who would be tending to our baby. We prayed for Jamie to come through the surgery safely, as well as for Bob and me to have the strength to tend to her during her recuperation. At that time, I just hadn't thought of asking for healing, but I was very grateful for a dedicated, godly woman who did.

I flew back to Joplin on Monday and took several snapshots of Jamie and her nice head of hair so I could remember what she looked like before they shaved it off. She would also be left with large scars on her skull. Bob, Jamie, and I met with the Neurosurgeon one last time before her operation. They took more X-rays so they would know exactly where to cut for her surgery. During the operation, they would need to shave her head, saw the bones in two, and insert some mesh pieces that would dissolve in a couple of years so the bones could fuse together as they were designed to do around the age of two.

When the X-rays were developed, the surgeon asked us to step into his office, where he could speak to us privately. We didn't know what to expect, since he had already gone over the surgical procedure in detail. We had made all the necessary arrangements for Jennifer and Jill. Plenty of blood had been donated in Jamie's name, and the Shriners had agreed to pay for all the costs. I felt we were as prepared as we possibly could be under the circumstances.

Bob and I walked into the doctor's office, where he had Jamie's X-rays displayed. Her new images, as well as her first X-rays, were up on the viewing screen. The surgeon got very excited as he pointed to her current X-rays. He said that he didn't know why, but Jamie's bones had opened, and she would no longer need the surgery. Bob and I knew why. God had healed her! God had healed our baby! This was a miracle! We were overcome with emotion and cried immensely. This was a lot to take in.

Words could never begin to express all the feelings Bob and I were going through. We were relieved that our baby didn't have to go through the surgery. We were honored and blessed that God chose to heal our child. There was absolutely no other explanation that anyone could ever give as to why a baby's bones were totally sealed shut one day and then opened the next, other than a true miracle. We gave all the praise and glory to God alone! We called to thank our friends and family for their prayers and to share the wonderful news of God's miracle. God blessed us in a way that we could never even imagine. Praise God; miracles still happen today!

In God's Word, it says, "Now to Him who is able to do immeasurably more than all we ask or imagine, according to His power that is at work within us" (Ephesians 3:20, NIV).

CHAPTER 10
A FRESH START
1981

We had made it! It was May of 1981, and Bob had completed his studies at Ozark Bible College to qualify to get his bachelor's degree in sacred literature. (BSL) We mailed out graduation announcements and were counting down the days until he received his diploma. To Bob and I, this meant much more than getting a diploma. We felt an enormous victory—we had not let Satan convince us of quitting when things got tough. We endured having two babies with no insurance to help pay the bills, Bob's double broken leg, unemployment, my health problems, the accident I sustained while seven months pregnant with Jamie, and almost pure financial disaster. That is just to name a few of the hardships we encountered during our four years at Bible college. God is victorious!

We were now looking forward to our future with great anticipation. Bob had a preaching ministry lined up at the Kirklin Christian Church in Kirklin, Indiana, where we'd have regular income, health insurance, a retirement plan, and a parsonage provided for us. Going back to Indiana was like going home for us. Kirklin was less than an hour away from Indianapolis, where all our relatives lived. We were excited!

The members of the church had the parsonage freshly painted and immaculately cleaned, awaiting our arrival. We were thrilled to have a house to live in once again instead of the trailer we called our home for four years. The backyard was fenced, so I didn't have to worry about the girls playing outside. Bob had less than a mile to drive to work each day. We felt truly blessed. Since we had been through such hard times in the past few years, we felt as though we had a much brighter future. Surely things would never be that bad again. Little did I know that I needed to hold on to my hat, as I was headed for the ride of my life in the years to come.

Bob worked feverishly in his new ministry. We wanted to get to know the members of the church as well as the townspeople. Kirklin was a small farming town with a population of around eight hundred people. We started many new friendships and seemed to be accepted well in the community. It was a nice feeling to be part of a town instead of being secluded on a college campus.

We had only been in Kirklin for a few weeks when it was time for the annual Kirk's Krossing weekend. The festival had carnival rides, talent shows, bingo, game booths, and their famous pork chop dinner. There was even a young queen named each year who rode in the town's fire truck during the Saturday morning parade. Our Jennifer was named queen, and she was one excited little girl.

On Sunday afternoon, during Kirk's Krossing, a special event is held called Sunday in the Park. Anyone who wanted to join in would bring their own picnic lunch. After eating, there were several other activities. Our family enjoyed the entire weekend.

All weekend, there were many drawings, where people could win prizes donated by local merchants. Jennifer won a toaster, and I won a two-liter bottle of pop and a bag of chips. Kyle Kercheval, a young man from our congregation, won a ham, and another family from our church won a pizza. We decided that it would be fun to invite those sitting around us that day to the parsonage the following weekend. Each person would bring the food they had won at Kirk's Krossing, along with their families, and we would share a fun evening of food and fellowship.

When I extended the invitation, Kyle and his younger brother Kent seemed surprised that Bob and I would ask anyone over to the parsonage. I soon found out that many of the former ministers at our church had not wished the parsonage to have an open welcome mat. I was more than thrilled to have people over and looked forward to getting to know each family better.

I loved having people in our home and was very excited to host our first guests. The Kercheval family, along with other families, joined us for an entertaining evening. I especially enjoyed getting to know Kyle and Kent's mother, Wanda. This was the beginning of a wonderful relationship that we still enjoy today. She is a delightful woman who was a prime example of a very dedicated mother of four boys. The joy and pride Wanda had in her sons was obvious. In the years to come, she would come to play a very important role in my life.

Later that summer, Bob took several of the men from our church with him to the Northmen retreat in Michigan. The girls and I stayed home and carried on with our normal routine. Jill had recently been diagnosed with asthma, and her doctor seemed concerned that it would not stay under control, even with all the medication she was taking. He scheduled Jill to be tested at St. Vincent's hospital for cystic fibrosis. The hours of waiting for answers seemed grueling. This must have been how my mother felt while she was waiting for the results about me when I was seventeen years old. It is very draining on a parent to wait for something that will impact a child's future.

Praise God, the results were negative, and I was absolutely thrilled. We still needed to deal with the severity of her asthma, but I was grateful that she didn't have cystic fibrosis.

Jill's doctor prescribed a nebulizer. We needed to learn how to prepare her medications in order to operate the machine four times each day. This meant that we would need to take the machine with us if we were going to be gone from our house for more than a few hours. It was very awkward at first, but it soon became part of our daily routine.

Many people asked me how I coped when I had one child in kindergarten, a two-year-old with severe asthma, a baby, my own health problems, and a new ministry. I realized that I didn't stop to think about those things. It was the life I was given, and I carried on the best way I knew.

I never thought anything about having to run Jill's machine on a daily basis, because I would have done whatever it took to take care of my child. This does not mean that there weren't days where I got tired or frustrated; it just meant that I prayed for guidance and strength to make it through another day.

I could never imagine having to deal with life's problems without knowing God was right there with me. I learned to pray constantly. I didn't just pray at mealtimes or at bedtime. I prayed while washing the dishes, running Jill's nebulizer, making the beds, or running the vacuum. Any time is a good time to pray.

God tells us in I Thessalonians 5:17–18, "Pray continually; give thanks in all circumstances, for this is God's will for you in Christ Jesus" (NIV). In Philippians 4:6–7, we are told, "Do not be anxious about anything, but in everything, by prayer and petition, with thanksgiving, present your requests to God. And the peace of God, which transcends all understanding, will guard your hearts and your minds in Christ Jesus" (NIV).

CHAPTER 11

MY CHILDREN NEED A MOTHER

1981

Jill's asthma was becoming more stabilized, but I noticed myself tiring quickly. I was having more trouble with my myasthenia gravis. Our calendar was quite booked during the month of September, and I tried to keep up with a grueling schedule. On Tuesday, the 29th, the ladies from our church took a shopping trip to Nashville, Indiana. Nashville is mainly a tourist town where there are stores full of homemade crafts and delectable restaurants.

An entire day of walking was exhausting. After arriving home from Nashville, I made dinner and then went to my room to rest for a while. Later that evening, after we put the girls to bed, I called a babysitter to come over so we could do our grocery shopping. Bob and I had been too busy over the weekend to get it done, and the pantry looked mighty bare.

It was raining like crazy as we drove into town. We noticed a truck in the ditch on the side of the road. Bob pulled over and stopped to see if we could help. A lady got out of the truck and started walking towards us. We asked her if she needed an ambulance. She said she wasn't hurt but would need a ride home. She got inside our car, and we exchanged introductions. She told Bob the directions to her home. When we arrived at her house, Bob gave her one of his business cards so she would have our phone number to call us if there was anything else we could do. She thanked us for our kindness, and we continued with our shopping trip.

The following night at Bible Study, I grew increasingly weak. I did not want to interrupt Bob's teaching, so I sat there in my chair, hoping I would be fine. I took some medicine for my MG, but it didn't seem to help. I finally reached a point where I felt I had no choice but to leave the room before I collapsed in front of everyone in attendance. I reached the back door of the church, where a member asked me if I was all right. I remember saying that everything was going black, and then I collapsed on the floor.

According to what I was told later, someone went to find Bob. He and Jay Hawley, one of our elders, got me into our car, and they drove me home. The two of them carried me into the house, and Bob put me in bed. Bob knew I had been extremely tired lately and figured that I probably needed some rest. He gave me some more Mestinon to see if that would help.

Bob walked back into the living room to thank Jay for his help. Jay had never witnessed me in this condition before and was quite concerned. He did not feel comfortable leaving and asked Bob to check on me one more time. Whether God prompted Jay, I don't know, but because of Jay's request to see me one more time, my life was saved. When Bob opened the bedroom door, they found that I had stopped breathing. Jay phoned the paramedics to report the situation. The ambulance arrived at our house almost immediately, since they were stationed just down the street. The medics performed CPR as they rushed me to St. Vincent hospital in Indianapolis. By the time the ambulance arrived at the hospital, my heart had stopped beating, and the staff at the hospital attempted to do a sternum rub and chest compressions to bring back a heartbeat. The staff in the emergency room took over from the paramedics and placed me on a respirator.

Eventually, I became conscious again. Since I was intubated and on life support, I was unable to talk. The tubes down my larynx were extremely painful, and I wanted them pulled out. I kept making the motions for someone to take out the tubes, but they kept telling me that they couldn't. The nurse explained to me that I was not breathing on my own—that I just felt like I was, because the machine was breathing for me. I became very agitated and didn't believe what she was saying. My nurse could see that I was not satisfied with her answer, so she told me to watch the monitor as she unhooked my tubing from the respirator. The needle fell down to zero. The shock of watching the calculating needle fall to nothing hit me extremely hard. I was scared. I had three little girls at home who depended on me. They needed their mother. I wasn't afraid of dying; I was concerned for my children.

Bob said a prayer to thank God for our family and the blessings He had bestowed upon us. Then he asked God for His divine intervention—that He would reverse the impact of the damages done to my body so that my health could be restored, at least until the girls were grown and out of school. He requested God's wisdom to be given to the doctors and nurses tending to me. He said he pleaded—not for himself, but for the girls and for me—that God would intervene.

The hospital contacted my parents in Iowa to notify them of my condition. The caller told my mom and dad that they needed to come as quickly as possible, since the doctors weren't sure if I would make it through the night—especially since they had lost me once already. There weren't any more flights out that evening going to Indianapolis, so they had to make the trip by car. It normally takes eight hours to get from Des Moines to Indianapolis, but God was with them as they sped to Indiana as fast as they could.

I was put in the intensive care unit and was only allowed to have family members visit for ten minutes every two hours. The nurse woke me in the early morning hours to let me know that my parents had arrived. Since they had driven such a long distance, they were allowed to stay with me longer than the allotted time. It was hard for them to see me in that condition—hooked up to life support.

Ministers didn't have to follow the normal visiting rules and were allowed to visit the patients at any time. When the next shift of nurses came on duty, Bob told them that he was my minister. This was technically true, but soon they wondered why he was being a little too friendly with the patient. After admitting that he was also my husband, they wrote on the front of my chart in big letters, "Pam's minister is her husband."

I had been in the hospital many times before, but this was the first time I had a male nurse. I was a little uncomfortable with that, but when you are hooked up to a ventilator, you don't have much say in the matter. Before this, I had never heard of a male nurse.

The next day, I had many visitors. Kyle Kercheval and Linda Fausset from our church told the nurses that they were family members so they would be able to get into the ICU to see me. My regular family members took turns sitting by my bedside every two hours. It was hard to allow others see me this way. I just wanted to be well and home with my girls.

On the third evening, several of the church members came to the hospital. The nurses decided to let them all in at once. I just remember seeing a bunch of people standing at the end of my bed. One lady had recently informed me that she had leukemia. I started crying when I caught a glimpse of her. I could not believe that she would take the time to drive into town to see me when she had just learned of her own serious health condition. When the nurses saw that I was crying, they asked everyone to leave, because they thought it was upsetting me to have so many people there.

On my fourth day in ICU, I had improved enough that I was able to be taken off the vent. I was breathing on my own! The nurses informed me that they would see how my day progressed, and maybe I could be admitted to a regular room by that evening. But once I knew that I was breathing on my own, I made a plan to get out of there as fast as possible. No one was going to keep me from my children one second longer! I checked myself out of the ICU against medical advice. I was determined to go home!

I didn't have a normal voice for several days, as the intubation had severely irritated my throat. I slowly regained my strength and started walking a little at a time. I wasn't able to eat much, since I was too tired to chew. I became extremely bored recuperating within the four walls of my bedroom, although I thoroughly enjoyed receiving cards in the mail and phone calls to check on my progress. One evening, I received a call from the lady whose truck was stuck in the ditch the night before I ended up on the respirator. She said she saw the article in the newspaper that was written about me and couldn't believe it was about the same people who had helped her just a few days before. It is fascinating to see how God intertwines our lives.

After my mother went back to Iowa, there wasn't anyone to help in the evenings while Bob attended meetings at church, so Kyle Kercheval offered to come over. He helped take care of the girls and get them to bed on time, as Jennifer needed to get up for school each morning. After tucking in the girls, he sat in my room to keep me company until Bob came home. Sometimes we would talk, but many times, I wasn't even able to stay awake. It was a blessing to have someone I could depend on until I was well enough to resume my normal responsibilities.

I had only been out of the hospital for three weeks when my doctors readmitted me into the hospital for another two weeks. I was not progressing as they had hoped, and I became depressed. The emotional recovery from the MG crisis was distressing me more than the physical recovery. When I was first diagnosed with myasthenia gravis, my specialist informed me that MG could lead to a crisis, but it had never happened to me. Before that time, MG was a burden that I had to bear, but a crisis could mean death for me. My children were still young. Jennifer was five, Jill was twenty-three months, and Jamie was not even a year old yet. My children needed a mother. They needed me. I didn't want my life to end like this.

It was hard being separated from my girls again. Hospitals didn't allow any children under the age of fourteen to go into the patients' rooms. It was a good thing that I had shopped early for the upcoming birthdays of Jill and Jamie. Their birthdays were just around the corner, and their presents were already wrapped and hidden in my closet.

I felt worthless as a mother, since I couldn't even take care of my own children for almost two months. Jamie had recently learned to walk and was toddling around. It was very cute. We had been switching her from a bottle to a sippy cup. At this age, a child grows quickly and is constantly learning new things. I didn't want to miss out on all those special moments. My Aunt Donnie took care of Jamie during my hospitalization and recovery and Jill stayed with my in-laws. Several of the families from our congregation helped with Jennifer since she needed to go to school. I was so grateful to have such wonderful family and friends to help during difficult times.

After thinking that we were on a new and exciting chapter in our lives since Bob's graduation from Bible college, I wondered if I would ever be able to help others when I was totally depending on them to assist me. It was difficult being a minister's wife who was on the receiving end. I wanted to be out there, serving the people of our church and others.

The myasthenia gravis had gone into what is known as the brittle stage. It was hard to regulate my medicine. A slight variation in the Mestinon could mean either an overdose or an under-dose. Both could lead to a crisis. It was like playing Russian roulette with my medication and my life.

Have you ever been at a point in your life where you wondered what would happen next? In Matthew 6:34, Jesus tells us, "Do not be anxious for tomorrow, for tomorrow will take care of itself. Each day has enough trouble of its own" (NASB). I began to rely on Scriptures for comfort. Many times, they would help me not to feel alone. God used this time to teach me patience and to rely on Him. Hebrews 11:1 reveals that "Faith is the assurance of things hoped for, the conviction of things not seen" (NASB). I was definitely hoping to be well, but it didn't look humanly possible for this to happen. There was one muscle that was tremendously strengthened during this time—my faith muscle!

CHAPTER 12

ONLY YOUR HAIRDRESSER
KNOWS FOR SURE

1983–1984

We had recently moved to a small town in southern Louisiana when I got the urge to do something different with my hair. I was browsing through the local newspaper when I found an advertisement with a coupon for two dollars off a haircut. The beauty shop was located only three miles from my house, so I thought this surely must have been an opportunity from God.

I called the phone number on the ad to schedule an appointment. I received a friendly greeting from a lady with a very thick Southern accent. I told her that I was calling about the coupon I found in the newspaper. She informed me that she was closed that day, but agreed to take me anyway as long as I didn't object to her wearing shorts. Upon arriving at her shop, I found a delightful and bubbly Cajun woman named Pat Oubre. She asked me to call her Miss Pat, since that was the proper way to address a lady there in the Deep South. Miss Pat's accent was so heavy that I didn't completely understand everything she was saying. I did not mind, though, as her cheerfulness quite made up for any misunderstanding.

We discussed my hair and what cut I would like. As she was cutting my hair, we visited the entire time and seemed to click from the very first moment. I left her shop that day excited about my new haircut, and also excited about making a new friend in town. Later that week, when I called her, we had a good laugh over how she forgot to take my coupon and give me the discount! No one else even called about the coupon that was in the newspaper. Little did Miss Pat or I imagine how God would use this newfound friendship as a tool for me to minister to her spiritual needs and she to minister to my physical needs in the days to come. God does work in mysterious ways!

Our friendship grew with each succeeding appointment. Our children also became acquainted, as they shared lunch in the school cafeteria. I extended Miss Pat an invitation to join me and several other women on Wednesday mornings for a Bible Study that I was teaching in my home. She declined, because she had many recurring customers who came to her shop on Wednesdays.

At my next hair appointment with Miss Pat, she seemed to be studying me. She wanted to know what was so different about me and my family. She went on to state how her family went to Mass each week and the children went to catechism classes, but there was something different about the closeness that Bob and I shared with our girls. Miss Pat thought that we seemed to have an openness when we talked about God in our lives. She asked me point-blank for the answer. I shared with her the personal relationship we had with Jesus Christ and that we studied God's Word.

A few weeks later, Miss Pat rearranged the days she kept her beauty shop open and asked about coming to my Bible study. I had just finished the series I was teaching at that time. I offered to study with her privately. She was amazed that anyone would consider taking the time to study with her personally. I told her that I would be more than happy to.

God had definitely sent me a challenge, as Miss Pat had recently remarried, and together, she and her husband were raising five children. My phone rang almost daily with questions regarding scriptural answers to everyday questions. I didn't always have the response right off the top of my head, but made sure I got back to her with answers after doing research on her questions. This caused me to dig deeper into God's Word, so it became a great learning experience for us both.

Our relationship continued to grow, and we were spending quite a bit of time together. Our girls arranged play dates with each other and even had sleepovers. Her oldest daughter, Monica, babysat whenever I had engagements that required me to leave the girls at home.

Miss Pat taught me how to cook using Cajun recipes, and I taught her how to make some Yankee recipes that she had never attempted before. One day, after teaching her how to make homemade noodles, the kids came home from school and wanted to know what we were doing. I told them that we were making noodles. One of her stepsons asked, "What are noodles?" She didn't quite know how to explain this type of pasta, so she told him to think of noodles as fat spaghetti!

Miss Pat and I ran our errands together, went to doctor's appointments with each other, and fixed the kids after-school snacks. We soon began spending most of our free time together. I decided that it was time to share with Miss Pat that I had myasthenia gravis. I described how the MG was a muscle disease and that different muscles could collapse at any time. I explained that I was diagnosed at the age of seventeen, had been pretty stable in the past year or so, but was again showing signs that I was getting weaker. I felt she should know about the MG in case I collapsed.

Throughout the summer, I kept losing weight, no matter how much I ate. I weighed less than one hundred pounds, and it wasn't easy finding clothes that fit. Many times, I had to shop in the children's department, or Miss Pat would help me sew some new outfits.

I felt my energy level dropping almost daily, and I thought maybe some vitamins would help. The fall semester of school would start in a few days, and it was the first day of school for my youngest daughter, Jamie. I wanted it to be special for her, so I cooked a big breakfast and took some pictures. She was only four and starting kindergarten. In Louisiana, kindergarten was a full day of class. The school bus picked up all three of the girls right in front of our home. I kissed Jennifer, Jill, and Jamie and waved goodbye as I watched them get on the bus.

I walked inside the house to get myself ready for a lunch date which several of my girlfriends and I planned to celebrate the kids' first day back to school. We were all meeting at my favorite Mexican restaurant in New Iberia, Tampico's, at 11:00 a.m.

While I was getting dressed, I felt a burning sensation on my face and a tingling running down my arms. This was very strange, and I couldn't imagine why it was happening. We had planned this luncheon over a week ago, and I wasn't going to let anything stop the great day. I figured that if it was a reaction to the vitamins I was taking, then it would soon go away.

Miss Pat phoned to see if I was ready, and I informed her of my current condition. She was concerned, since I had recently told her about my MG. She remembered me saying how remissions and relapses can occur at any time. Nothing like this had ever happened before, so I wasn't quite sure what to tell her. I was, however, starting to get very weak.

She told me that she was stopping by to pick up a neighbor, and they would be right over.

My condition deteriorated greatly before their arrival. Miss Pat and Miss Suzette assessed the situation and decided that I needed to get to my doctor right away. The two women attempted to pick me up and carry me out to the car. Even though I only weighed around one hundred pounds, it was pure dead weight. As they were trying to lug me through the front door, they banged my body against the wall and almost dropped me. Miss Pat started laughing hysterically, as she often did when she got nervous. This must have been a sight!

It was a twenty-minute drive into town, and by that time, I wasn't even able to talk. Miss Pat could only remember the name of one of my doctors, so they drove me to Dr. Blue's office. There was only one problem—he was my gynecologist. He didn't know what to do, so he looked through my chart to find out who was my primary care physician. He phoned the office of Dr. Ditch and asked him to meet us at the hospital.

In the meantime, my other friends were waiting at the restaurant for us to arrive. They couldn't imagine why we weren't there, since this was our big day to celebrate, and I would never miss it. Miss Andrea called my house, and there was no answer, so she figured we were on our way but running late. The girls asked the waiter if he would go ahead and show them to a table. They snacked on chips and salsa while waiting. Thirty more minutes passed, and there was still no word from us. By this time, they figured something terrible must be wrong, and they caught up with us at the hospital. I never did get to hear if they ever ate lunch!

I had a reaction to the vitamins, all right, but it caused me to go into a myasthenic crisis. This time, I only had to spend one night and was able to go home the next day after being stabilized. This was a big relief for me, since a few years earlier, I had to be put into the ICU and on a respirator for several days.

The MG was back in full force. My remission was over, and I was to experience the myasthenia gravis in the stages my specialist had told me about when I was first diagnosed as a teenager. I was back on large doses of my medication. I felt like I was on a roller coaster ride going faster and faster; I just wanted to get off.

It wasn't long before walking around my house became a big challenge. A wheelchair became my companion. Miss Pat stopped by daily to check on me. Many times, she took me—along with my wheelchair—into town just so I could get out of the house. It wasn't an easy task for her, but she knew how much it meant to me. She was quite a friend!

I love to help others, and I couldn't even make it through the day without the help of someone else. How could I minister to Miss Pat when the muscles in my mouth wouldn't allow me to talk for any length of time? I couldn't even eat without choking. The one I was witnessing to was now helping me pull down my pants so I could use the bathroom. I prayed, "Lord, how can this be to your glory?"

God uses others as His instruments, and He was teaching me some mighty big lessons. Each day, I grew more frustrated physically. My husband would bathe me, brush out my hair, get breakfast for the family, and get the girls off to school—all before leaving for work each day. Miss Pat or one of the women from our church would bring lunch, make dinner, and do some laundry and light housekeeping. Allowing others to tend to *my* needs was a hard lesson to learn and accept.

I shared my frustrations with Miss Pat, and her response became a message that I would never forget. She explained that she understood how hard all of this must be for me, but I needed to understand how the people who were tending to my needs were feeling. She said, "You don't realize how hard it is to watch your friend slipping away before your eyes. You continue to get weaker, and you can't even eat without choking. We wonder whether you will even make it through the next crisis. We feel so helpless. Don't you understand—it at least helps us if we can tend to your physical needs? We need to feel like we are helping in some way." I had not put myself in their shoes, so I prayed that God would help me see the hurts of others also involved in my situation.

My health continued deteriorating during the next several weeks. I was having one MG crisis after another, but my spiritual life was blossoming. God spoke to me in mighty and strong ways. Certain Scriptures would almost leap off of the pages of His Word. Two verses that were particularly meaningful at this time were Philippians 4:13, "I can do all things through Christ who gives me strength," and II Corinthians 12:9–10, "My grace is sufficient for you for my power is made perfect in weakness. For when I am weak, then I am strong" (NIV).

Miss Pat and others continued to meet my physical needs, and I shared the love of Christ with them. Many years have passed since this struggling time, but the lessons that God taught me from this experience were never lost. I no longer live in Louisiana, but Miss Pat and I still visit and talk to each other on a regular basis. She uses God's teachings in her own life and also shares these principles with others.

Never doubt God's ability to use any situation for His glory. I've learned to always leave myself open to God's teachings. You never know how God will use you or who God will use to work in your life. Who could have imagined that God would use the experience of a hairdresser and the new girl in town?

CHAPTER 13

I'M SORRY, THERE'S NOTHING MORE WE CAN DO

1985–1986

The Mestinon was no longer keeping my myasthenia stable. I started having many Myasthenic crises. Since we lived over twenty minutes from the nearest hospital, the doctors taught Bob how to inject the tensilon, the shot that would make my muscles react immediately. As far as we knew, I was the only MG patient in America who kept the tensilon with her at all times. Normally, it would only be administered by a physician in the emergency room. A crisis would come on so quickly that I no longer had enough warning to get to a hospital in time.

One night, Bob sat beside me on the bed, studying. I had lost control of all my muscles and couldn't even make enough noise to alarm him. I knew he thought I had fallen asleep. There was one thing I didn't lose when all my muscles collapsed—the ability to pray. Praise God, He knows our thoughts. I had never before been so thankful to comprehend that God can hear us whether or not we pray out loud. It would require prompting from the Lord for Bob to check on me. Bob leaned over, saw that I was in crisis, and took the proper action required. God's will was done, and I pulled through once more.

My husband and I knew our time together was very precious. Each morning, he set the alarm half an hour before he needed to get up for work just so we could spend some quality time together. It became hard for Bob to go to work each day when he wondered if I would still be alive when he came home at night.

Time was a precious commodity, and it didn't matter if I was surrounded by gold and riches, as *things* were not going to make me well. My biggest fear was that the girls would come home from school to find me dead. It was bad enough that they had witnessed an ambulance hauling me away to the hospital on several occasions. I didn't want that to be their last memory of me.

Autumn had arrived—and along with it, my seasonal hay fever. It was miserable being so congested, and soon the congestion developed into a sinus and upper respiratory infection which aggravated the MG. Miss Pat took me to see Dr. Ditch. He gave me a prescription to treat the infection, but was really at a loss for anything else to do regarding the myasthenia.

Later that afternoon, my doctor called me at home and said, "I'm sorry, there is nothing more I can do. Try not to get anxious about it."

I was almost yelling when I responded, "Try not to get anxious about it? I have three girls to raise and more life to live!" I asked him to please call my MG specialist in Indianapolis, Dr. Tether, to consult with him.

Dr. Ditch did call Dr. Tether, and they came up with a plan. Since the Mestinon didn't seem to be holding anymore and I was so brittle, a choice had to be made. He discussed a thymectomy with me, but there was no guarantee of a reversal or remission. With my infection and my condition deteriorating so rapidly, they weren't sure I could survive the surgery anyway. He did say there was one other thing they could try. Medical research started showing some good results with steroid therapy in other critical MG patients.

We could try the steroids, but I had to understand the side effects they could impose on my body if I chose to take them. Dr. Ditch gave me some information to read about taking prednisone. We read the documents diligently.

The literature I was given stated that I would gain weight and have a large, round, moon-shaped face. I could end up with Glaucoma, cataracts, and diabetes. It could wear away at my bones and destroy organs in my body—not to mention the emotional roller coaster it would put me on. How could this be my only choice? If I didn't start the steroid therapy, the next crisis could be my last; but if I did, then I could end up with many other medical conditions in the years to come.

Bob and I talked it over. To me, there was only one choice. I chose to live, which meant choosing the prednisone—even with all its possible side effects. I had always been one who had goals, and my goal was to stay alive and watch my girls grow up.

Dr. Ditch started me out on a small dose every other day along with my Mestinon. I had much to learn about the steroid use, and some of it would be learned the hard way. I wasn't eating much during this time, because it was too much effort, and I hated choking on even the simplest of things, like ice cream. No one bothered to tell me that you needed to eat before taking the prednisone. I became extremely nauseous. There is one thing I cannot stand to do—vomit. Luckily, there was an easy remedy to this problem. If only all of our problems in life could be this easy to fix!

I kept a calendar by my bedside to help keep me organized. I marked every other day with an X to know when to take the prednisone along with my Mestinon. Since starting the steroids, I began retaining fluid and therefore needed a diuretic. My anxiety level was tremendous, and I had to take a prescription for that. The headaches and pain in my legs caused me to take several pain medications on a regular basis. The medical bills were mounting, and I hated knowing that it was costing Bob everything he had just to keep me alive. I wanted to be there for my girls, but I felt guilty because of the expense. That became an emotional nightmare for me.

On the days I needed to take the steroids, I wasn't able to sleep, since they made me so hyper. Luckily, a girlfriend of mine, Vivian, was a night owl, and she stayed up, talking to me on the phone until I was able to fall asleep.

I had good days and bad ones. I did not know from one day to the next whether I would be totally bedridden or able to carry on with my household chores. I could feel good in the mornings but be at the mercy of others by the afternoon. My health became so fragile that I could be talking to a friend one minute and be on the floor, unable to move, the next.

I became very discouraged and went into depression. The doctors told me that it was common for someone who has a chronic illness to become depressed, but it was very upsetting to me. I once had a body which could play sports, run, jump, and keep up with the best of them. Then I had a body whose muscles didn't function to their capacity, and sometimes my body didn't allow me to even walk to the bathroom on my own, drive a car, tend to my family, or even go to church. Many times, I could not move any muscle, which meant that I couldn't yell for help or even reach for the phone to dial 911. In those times that I could not move, I was still conscious and could hear those around me talking about me as if I wasn't there. The only reason that I knew I was alive was because I could think and pray. Psalm 46:10 says, "Be still and know that I am God" (NIV). I sincerely identified with that Scripture. God was the only one I was able to communicate with.

I would pray for the Lord's will to be done. If it was God's will that I continued living, He would need to make available a trained person who knew how to tend to a Myasthenic crisis. They would need to stabilize me before the muscles in my throat collapsed and I lost my airway passage. During these times, I understood perfectly that God was in control. *I could do nothing.* In these critical moments, I learned about being dependent on God and His magnificent grace and mercy.

It was October, and my health continued to decline, but my two youngest daughters, Jill and Jamie, had birthdays. They were turning six and five, respectively. I wanted to give them a birthday party, but I spent most of my time in bed or in my wheelchair. My walking mainly consisted of getting to the bathroom or the kitchen on my good days. At that time, I wasn't sure of the longevity of my life, but I was certain that I wanted to create loving memories for my children.

It wasn't easy to orchestrate party plans from my bed, but I had terrific friends who wanted to help. Many people tried to talk me out of having the party, saying that the girls would understand. I knew in my heart that this was something I wanted and needed to do.

During the month of October, the temperature is still very warm outside in southern Louisiana, so we were able to hold the party in the backyard. My friends hung the decorations, and Bob played games with the children. There seemed to be plenty of laughing, clapping, and jumping up and down, so I felt the children were all having a great time. Jill and Jamie blew out the candles on their cake and opened their presents. The guests all shared in the cake and ice cream. I sat in a chair inside the house by the sliding glass door so I could watch the party unfold. I wanted to see the smiles on Jill and Jamie's faces as the day progressed. The girls thanked me for giving them a party.

After all the guests had gone home, Jennifer helped her dad take down the decorations and put the presents away. The girls took their baths and were tucked in for the night. My goal was complete. I don't even remember the presents we bought them that year, but I do remember the labor of love and the memories that were created that day. Things shall come and go, but memories will last a lifetime. Twelve years later, Jamie was asked to create a story for her class at school. She wrote about "the miracle family." Her story was about when I had a birthday party for her and her sister while I was very sick. It really tugged at my heart to see that it had created a memory for her with a lasting impact.

A woman from our church told me that she had written a poem that she wanted to give me. Pam enjoyed writing poems and said she was moved by my dedication, even while I was ill. She overheard me make the comment one day that I didn't want to become a burden to my family. Below is the poem Pam Pegg wrote about my life. It is written from my perspective and also the perspectives of my husband, daughters, fellow sisters in Christ, and God.

BURDEN
Pam Pegg

Burden, I've been so sick. Too sick too long.
Burden, always asking, always needing. Having to
ask for help; I don't want to be a burden.
Beggared by my health, I want to give to others,
but it seems I always have to take.
I hate the asking, hate the begging, hate the
needing.
If will alone could heal, then I'd be whole. If will
alone could kill, I might be dead.
I hate it so, but I'm alive. I'm still alive. My need
goes on. Why?

Burden Darling? You're my wife, my life. If it
were me, you'd willingly. But it is you, and what
you need, I give; I must supply. My other half,
Soul Mate. Just as I breathe, no burden that.

Burden Mama. Sure, there are many things we
cannot do and things we do for you.
The other kids don't understand. We're learning
love; that's more than words. Love that sacrifices.
You do for us.

A birthday party when you knew how much it
hurts you. Yet you smiled.
Your love for us, we love you too. Together, we
will take care of you.
Together, we'll take care of us, and we will
understand that Love is you.

Burden Sister? Don't you see how doing for you
brings relief to me?
My heart loads down each day with petty
worries magnified by closeness. Helping you adds
perspective again. Makes them small again.

I know you don't believe it, feeling each new fear,
but you are brave, you have to be.
That helps my trust in God to grow, my fears to die.
Remember, Sister, giving is more blessed, so
giving to you gives me the blessings that you can't
see, since your receiving; you're my opportunity.
Sister, you teach, you give in all you are. We love
you for that. What you are.

Burden daughter? Burden to them? In some small
ways, perhaps. Late suppers, missed treats, delayed
plans. Yes, they're inconveniences.
From my Heaven, I see you as you see yourself—
broken, parasitic. Being your Father, I know
what you are. Yes, you're human. Flawed as every

human is. Clothed within my dear Son's blood. Saved eternally.

I also see you through their eyes. I know what you mean to them. Listen, and I'll share with you their care.
To my earthly family, you teach perspective, bravery, and faith. To your daughters, you are love. And to your husband, you are life. A burden? Only one of love. Love's burdens are the lightest stuff.

Why? Ah, daughter, for all of Job's patience, I never told him why I let him suffer so. When you come home, we'll open the Book, and there'll be reasons all explained.
Meanwhile, glimpses come your way—good that's done. Good that becomes because of you.
Enjoy the glimpses, and remember—you are many things, my daughter, valuable to all who help you. Giving things unseen, immeasurable. I've the strength you need, Just lean.
You cannot lean too hard on Me.

Love burden Daughter, always light, always easy, always a blessing.

★★★

My mother phoned to wish the girls happy birthday. Afterwards, she wanted to talk to me. She could hear the weakness in my voice. She felt that we needed to get in touch with my specialist in Indianapolis and schedule me to see him right away. My mother called me back the next day with my appointment. My local doctor, Dr. Ditch, did not feel that I was strong enough to fly home, so my friend, Vivian, who was originally from Indianapolis herself, agreed to drive me there in her van. This gave me the opportunity to lie down during the trip. Vivian understood myasthenia, since her sister was also dealing with it. There was great comfort when someone understood what I was going through. I didn't need to be strong for them, and I could experience the anguish in that season of my life.

After we arrived in Indianapolis, I went to see Dr. Tether. He was very alarmed about the critical state I was in. He raised the amount of steroids I was taking to 100 mg, and I needed to continue on the large amounts of Mestinon. He warned me to be extremely cautious about being around anyone who was ill. He said that if I were to get any type of infection, "That's all she wrote." Dr. Tether wasn't sure that I would be around to celebrate Christmas, but we were trying to do everything possible to alleviate my grave status.

I know Bob was anxious for me to get back to Louisiana to spend time with him and the girls, but I thought I ought to take advantage of the opportunity to visit all our relatives while I was already in Indianapolis. It was an extremely emotional time for me, since I wasn't sure that I would ever see any of them again. My parents had a difficult time letting me leave.

I made it back to Louisiana and worked diligently on regaining my strength and staying positive. We didn't want to frighten and overwhelm the girls, so we didn't say much to them about my recent visit with the MG specialist. They were very aware of how sick I was, so I only answered the questions they posed to me.

Since taking the increased doses of prednisone, I was gaining strength each day. It was nice being able to get around again by myself and spend time with Bob and the girls. I felt hopeful for the first time in a long time. We actually had several weeks during which I was fairly stable. I decorated the house for Christmas, and I wanted the holidays to be as normal as possible. I knew exactly what I wanted to give my three lovely daughters for Christmas. I bought them each a locket and put my picture on the inside. When they opened the lockets to see my picture, the necklaces played the song, "Let Me Call You Sweetheart."

A few weeks later, I came down with a double infection. I was in extreme pain and became dreadfully frail. The words Dr. Tether had said about me getting an infection echoed in my mind. Bob called everyone we could think of to ask for prayers on my behalf. We faithfully made our requests known to God, our heavenly Father. We petitioned for divine intervention one more time. I couldn't imagine not being there for my girls.

Many prayers to God, our heavenly Father, were sent to plead for my health. I felt blessed to have wonderful friends who also believed in the power of prayer. It took three rounds of antibiotics and six weeks' time, but I did conquer the infection! More than that, God chose to intervene. Prayers do make a difference.

I needed the assistance of the steroids for six more years, but during that time, I began driving again, resumed my wifely and motherly responsibilities, went back to college, and passed my state boards in radiography. I had beaten the odds; I went to school and had a career—and they said it couldn't be done.

Also during those six years is when I researched, studied, and learned everything I could on the personality temperaments. I read every book I could find, including several from Tim LaHaye and Florence Littauer. I even went to sessions to study directly from Florence. Eventually I took this concept to my sister who owned a Home Health Company and shared the information with her. I explained how these principles could be used to help her employees understand the many different doctors and patients that they would encounter. Eventually I taught day-long seminars to all her employees from the administrative staff to the field staff in her ten office locations within Indiana and Illinois. From there, I started teaching couples this fine art of getting along and understanding each other. I also spoke at churches and to teachers, and even provided private counseling sessions. God blessed each and every one of those classes. I received countless letters from people whose lives were changed after understanding the differences in people and their perspectives. Florence and Fred Littauer flew to Indiana to interview me and how I successfully used Florence's personality principles in the workplace. She used part of our interview in her book called, "Personality Puzzle".

Even after getting off the steroids, celebrating my birthday is more of an anniversary celebration—a victory of sustaining life beyond the doctor's expectations. One year, I climbed to the highest point of the Great Smoky Mountains. When I reached the top, I said, "If my doctors could only see me now!" The next year, on my birthday, I sent a letter to the doctor that said, "I'm sorry, but there is nothing more we can do" and told him of my mountaintop experience. Later that summer, Miss Pat ran into Dr. Ditch while running errands in town. He told her of receiving my letter and inquired about how I was doing. He was amazed to hear how well my health had progressed since I last saw him in 1985.

I have relocated to several different states and even a Third World country since my gravely ill status of myasthenia gravis. Each time I moved, I had to start all over with a new doctor and was required to fill out medical history forms. I had to request extra paper to write on, since there weren't enough blanks to list all of my surgeries, diagnosis, and medications. It wasn't uncommon for a doctor to read a copy of my medical history and proclaim that I was a true living miracle. Ephesians 1:19 says, "I pray that you will begin to understand the incredible greatness of His power for us who believe Him" (NLT). Isn't God great? All praise and glory goes to God in the highest!

CHAPTER 14
I KNOW HOW YOU FEEL
1984–2011

When confined to my bed, unable to move without the assistance of another, I really resented when a visitor would make the comment, "I know how you feel." Deep inside was a voice screaming, "You don't have a clue!"

Can people honestly say they can comprehend what it is like to be unable to hold your eyes open because the muscles in your eyelids are too tired? Do they know the feeling of waking up and wondering if they will be able to move their arms or legs that day? Can they grasp what it is like to choke every time they try to eat, because their muscles aren't strong enough to chew and swallow?

Did my bedside callers empathize with the depression that accompanies a chronic illness? I once had a body which could run, play sports, and climb stairs. Now my muscles don't always function as they should, which prevents me from doing normal daily activities for any length of time. Many times, I can't even yell out for help. This does bring about a sense of discouragement.

Did my visitors comprehend what it is like to have their children stand over them, crying because they couldn't wake them up? I could hear my children crying, trying desperately to get me to move, but I could not respond to them. There were many days when the girls would come home from school and sit on my bed with me to share about their day, since I could not get out of bed to play with them. Did my friends understand the guilt I feel over not being able to take my girls to attend events like other children? I desperately wanted to be able to function like the majority of healthy mothers who were involved in their children's lives.

My heart was willing, but my flesh was weak. I loved to work with other women and teach classes, but it was hard to make a commitment. I never knew if I would be strong enough to attend the class myself. Sometimes when I woke up in the morning, I couldn't open my eyes; yet I could sense that I was awake. I would pray for God's grace.

Just as it says in II Corinthians 12:9, "My grace is sufficient for you, for my power is made perfect in weakness" (NIV). II Corinthians 12:10 states, "This is why, for Christ's sake, I delight in weaknesses, in insults, in hardships, in persecutions, in difficulties. For when I am weak, then I am strong."

I didn't know from one day to the next—or many times, one hour to the next—how I would be feeling. A girlfriend had her baby and wanted to share that joy with me, but I didn't like holding someone else's child for fear I might drop the baby. I loved sharing meals at the homes of our friends, but found excuses not to help with the dishes. I couldn't risk wondering if while drying the fine china, my arms would suddenly collapse. Others did not grasp what it was like to be taking a walk with your children and worry if your legs would be strong enough to carry you back home.

I would rather have a person sit by my bedside and talk to me, pray for me, or offer to take my girls for a few hours than to say, "I know how you feel." Many had never even heard of myasthenia gravis, let alone identify what it was like to go through a Myasthenic crisis.

On the other hand, there is nothing more comforting than someone actually understanding exactly how I am feeling. If I knew that my guests had fared similar circumstances, it was a great consolation to believe that they actually comprehended my plight. If God had brought them through this type of adversity, then I wasn't the only person on the planet who had such strife. It was reassuring to know I wasn't alone. God would comfort me through those people.

II Corinthians 1:3–4: "Praise be to the God and Father of our Lord Jesus Christ, the Father of compassion and the God of all comfort, who comforts us in all our troubles, so that we can comfort those in any trouble with the comfort we ourselves have received from God" (NIV).

If it was God's will to use this thorn in my flesh for His glory, then use me, Lord! It would be twenty-three years before God would use me personally to comfort a family who was dealing with myasthenia gravis. Over the years, I had talked to many different people who had lost members of their family to MG, but God had not directly used me to help a family who was dealing with MG in the present moment until the spring of 2008.

We had recently moved to Huntsville, Texas, where my husband was a hospital administrator, and God used his ministry in mighty ways, but I needed a ministry of my own to be used by God. One day, as I was saying my prayers, I asked God for a specific assignment. I wanted Him to use *me* for His glory. I didn't know many people in town, so I wasn't sure how this assignment would come about, but I left myself open to be used as He saw fit. Never could I have imagined I would receive my assignment the following morning.

We lived in a community called Elkins Lake. Included in our neighborhood association fees was a clubhouse that was used to host many events. On the third and fourth Wednesday mornings of each month, I joined in the local Bunco group. Before we started to play, we filled out our lunch orders on tickets. After Bunco was over, we each went into the dining room and found our lunch tickets. We never knew who we would be sitting beside each week. That particular day, I was seated next to a very sanguine lady named Betty Lowe. We visited for a while, and then she proceeded to tell me about her husband's health condition. She seemed very concerned about him. Betty and John were getting very frustrated, because the doctors had run many tests but still could not figure out the cause of all his symptoms. She started describing them to me, and it took everything I had to keep from crying. I knew exactly what he had. He had myasthenia gravis, and I wouldn't wish that on anyone. I didn't say anything to Betty that day about what I was thinking, but I did tell her that I would ask my husband for a recommendation of a specialist they could try.

John and Betty took Bob's recommendation and went to see the doctor he suggested. The following week at Bunco, she couldn't remember what the doctor thought it might be, as it was something she had never heard of before, but that on John's next appointment, they would run a certain test to be sure. I asked her if they used words like synapses, receptor sites, and tensilon. Betty answered with a resounding "Yes!" I then told her what they thought it was—myasthenia gravis. I shared with her what to expect next. She was concerned, because after John's tests, they were leaving for their grandson's wedding ceremony, and she wanted to make sure that he would be feeling up to attending. I assured Betty that it would be fine. There were not any lingering side effects from the test. After his confirmed diagnosis, I spent many hours educating John and Betty on how to cope, as best they could, with this devastating muscle disease. John lived for another thirty months before he went to be with the Lord on December 10, 2010.

It was good to know that God could actually use me and everything I had gone through to help another family who was enduring the same thing. It was just like the Scripture said—God comforts us through *all* our troubles *so that* we can comfort those with the comfort we ourselves had been comforted with.

God has allowed me to go through many trials in my fifty-five years here on the earth, including health conditions and many other adversities, but now I am hoping that by sharing this journey, you too can know the wondrous grace, love, and comfort of our heavenly Father.

There have been many times of joy and of sorrow in my life, but I kept my faith, knowing God was right there with me. James 1:12 states, "Blessed is the man who perseveres under trial, because when he has stood the test, he will receive the crown of life that God has promised to those who love Him" (NIV).

As with one of the first verses that I discovered after my mountaintop adventure in Colorado, Romans 8:28 states, "And we know that God causes all things to work together for good to those who love God, to those who are called according to His purpose" (NASB).

I am thankful for God's continued blessings. I am also thankful that He was able to touch a variety of lives through my illness that might not have seen a glimpse of Jesus' love otherwise. To God be the glory!

HEALTH UPDATE AND AFTERWORD

As I finish writing this book in the summer of 2011, I am still in remission from the myasthenia gravis. Most of my current health issues stem from the side effects of the prednisone I chose to use in 1985 to extend my life. (Refer to chapter thirteen).

To date I have endured through 12 different surgical procedures, many of which they operated on more than one organ or body part at a time, and countless health conditions that keep me challenged, but I carry on with Christ as my strength. He is the source of all mercy and comfort. I continue to be blessed!

I am currently writing a second book that takes a look at how our family tackled many other obstacles that came our way; plus a third book about serving in a Third World country.

I can be reached through my email address:
Keepingthefaith19@att.net

While writing this book, Joplin, Missouri was hit by another tornado in which thirty percent of the town was flattened and the death toll has risen to over one hundred lives.

Please pray for this lovely town as they rebuild and pray for the families whose lives were forever changed.

May God continue to bless you and your families as you serve Him.

CPSIA information can be obtained at www.ICGtesting.com
Printed in the USA
240230LV00002B/1/P